ADVANCE PRAISE

Michael Hickins has written an acerbically funny and ultimately heart-wrenching Picaresque memoir in *The Silk Factory: Finding Threads of My Family's True Holocaust Story*. Beautifully observed details of a seemingly last-chance marriage and late-in-life fatherhood combine with a quest to right the Holocaust-era theft of a family business make for an entertaining and emotionally resonant page-turner. As we follow Hickins from America, where he has "managed the seemingly impossible... Laura, who loves me like no other, doesn't like me anymore," to Europe and a road trip accompanied by a motley group of sparring characters, he also takes us on another journey, that of transforming his own acute and self-destructive shortcomings into some chance of redemption. **A wonderful, deeply illuminating book to savor.**

—Alice LaPlante, New York Times bestselling author of *Turn of Mind, Half Moon Bay* and *The Making of a Story*.

The Silk Factory is a terrific read, a Holocaust book unlike any other. Hickins, a refreshingly honest memoirist, takes readers on a suspenseful journey, skillfully navigating hard questions both about Nazi crimes and his own life choices.

—Sam Apple, author of *Ravenous: Otto Warburg, the Nazis, and the Search for the Cancer-Diet Connection.*

By turns razor-sharp and heartbreakingly tender, Michael Hickins's memoir is **an unforgettable exploration of personal and intergenerational history—the traumas we inherit, the stories we tell ourselves and our children, and the stories that are hidden, even as they shape our lives. Above all,** *The Silk Factory* **is about the courage to seek the truth.**

—Dawn Raffel, author of *The Strange Case of Dr. Couney* and *Boundless as the Sky.*

What we know, what we will never know, are the tormenting and tangled concerns of children of refugees and survivors. Michael Hickins in his remarkable and intense memoir *The Silk Factory* deals complexly with fragments of his family's past as he wrestles with these questions. Yes, this is a historical journey where, with scant clues, Hickins uncovers the story of his family's factory and home stolen during the Holocaust (which still operates today) and the murder of his family members. But this is also a powerful and unflinching personal quest as Hickins bravely attempts to untangle the legacy of generational trauma, the corrosive sorrow and rage that has infected his childhood, his marriage, and his parenting.

—Victoria Redel, author of *Paradise.*

In this story from a Holocaust survivor's son, as he uncovers his past, as he learns about his family – learns so much that no one's ever told him – and shares with us as he learns, we learn from him, we see how that which was sundered remains broken, generation after generation. And decades later, the loss, the pain, lives on inside him too, his failed marriages, the rage that he can barely keep bottled up. But by the end of this story Hickins finds himself in a different place. As he puts it, "not forgiving yourself at all is the best way of passing the behavior down to future generations. I may be inexcusable, but I have to forgive myself for the sake of my children."

—Michael Gottlieb, author of *Mostly Clearing* and *The Voices*, and a founding member of the Language poetry school.

THE SILK FACTORY

FINDING THREADS OF MY FAMILY'S TRUE
HOLOCAUST STORY

MICHAEL HICKINS

ISBN 9789493276918 (ebook)

ISBN 9789493276895 (paperback)

ISBN 9789493276901 (hardcover)

Publisher: Amsterdam Publishers, The Netherlands

info@amsterdampublishers.com

The Silk Factory is part of the series Holocaust Heritage

Copyright © Michael Hickins 2023

Cover image: Alexander von Ness www.nessgraphica.com

Author photo: Alexandre Ayer

CONTENTS

1

HE ALSO LIVES IN THE HOUSE

Thurman, my first-born 29-year-old-son, is in the back seat of the fancier-than-we-could-afford rented metallic-blue Volvo c90, alongside the car seat cradling my three-year-old, Max, who is watching age-appropriate videos on my company phone, scarfing up data limits I will hear about from HQ when the bill comes due.

My wife Laura is next to me in the passenger seat, occasionally gripping the escape handle above her head as we barrel along the French portion of the A4 motorway towards Germany.

She's got reasons to be jumpier than usual – a rental car, a manual transmission I'm not used to driving, a harrowing speed limit, the suddenness of giant, diesel-belching lorries blaring past us, and a husband who wears his heart on his sleeve and a temper like a red pocket kerchief poking out of his breast pocket, and who is even more preoccupied than usual.

The highway pavement changes to a deeper black as we leave France and enter Germany, and the height and texture of the blacktop changes, a tiny, unnatural barrier reef that marks the national border and causes the Volvo to bump, and the tin box containing my mother's ashes to clunk in the cargo space behind us.

The rolling hills and high stands of skinny trees remain, but the road itself becomes sleeker, and the rest areas more utilitarian, less inviting. We learn that *"Ausfahrt"* means "exit," which makes us giggle like little children. And fortunately, the rest stops have hot dogs aplenty, which is all Max seems to need. That and watching Bob the Builder videos.

It is Monday morning, and we aren't due at the factory in Ansbach until early Tuesday afternoon, when we're scheduled to meet with Klaus Kalbkopf, the current chief executive of the family-run business for more than 135 years that is and isn't my family's business.

I'm 58, and I was dumbfounded a few months earlier to learn that the factory was even still in existence. I had believed that my father, his sister and mother had been forced to sell it because Jews weren't allowed to own property in Nazi Germany. That they had handed control of it over to my aunt's ex-husband, a Gentile named Reinhold Lutz, for safekeeping. Then, my parents glibly explained, life had intervened and they had all moved on after the war. My sister's ex-husband had remarried, my father's first wife drowned in Cuba, and they had put their energies into getting their lives back together as best they could. The factory itself, the house my father grew up in (and which was used as the company office), had dissolved into the fractal-glazed mists of history. I never thought about it, and had no reason to.

Then came the email from Luis, the nephew I never knew I had.

I'm keeping my eyes on the road and my fists clenched on the steering wheel, and I'm thinking ahead to what might happen in Ansbach – "thinking ahead" being a misnomer for "fantasizing about the future."

But never far from my mind is another thought, and one that comes back to me on the regular: "You've fucked this up. Again."

"This" being the central relationship of my life, and the fact that it has been become non-erotic and unromantic. Conjugal without the conjugations. Marital infertility. Connubial without much canoodling. I suspect Laura would have left me by now if we hadn't become parents (back when Eros, romance, and conjugations were intrinsic to our marriage).

Even in this rental car, evidence of my past and present fuckupitutde abounds: the slightly impatient sighing of my eldest son, a tall, handsome, dark-haired young man whom years ago I left behind with his French mother in France so I wouldn't have to separate from Liz, the American mother of my daughter Clara; and Clara, the slender, blue-eyed woman whose absence is almost tangible, and who isn't here because inviting her on this trip was an afterthought that worked out the way most afterthoughts do.

And then there's Laura, the emotionally wary woman at my right, still my wife, mother of Max.

I'm desperate – truly desperate – to not fuck this up any further, to somehow undo the fuckuptedness I feel I have created. I don't want to be a divorced dad – again – and I don't want to go through the wrenching pain of admitting that the love I so treasure is gone – and what's worse, by my own doing. Because I yell and shout and stomp my feet, and at six-foot-one, am an imposing, if ultimately nonviolent, Baby Huey.

I'm always waiting for the magic moment when Laura recalls what it was about me that made her feel sexually in love, in special love, specks-of-light-dancing-in-front-of-her-eyes love. But the more time passes, the more I feel this moment will never come, and each time I get that feeling, I turn – inexplicably-to-Laura – morose and glum, which is certainly not the spark she'd need to rekindle her specks of light.

So I vacillate between unspoken expectations of rekindled passion and monosyllabic despondency.

And if I do express myself, it's with a passive-aggressive line filled with self-pity, like, "I'm too young to never have sex again!"

Kalbkopf, the chief executive of what was once my family's silk factory, has graciously agreed to show me around the plant. I'm torn – I want to make it a friendly visit. I don't want to assert myself too much – not now. There is time enough for confrontations, perhaps even lawsuits.

Also, I don't want Kalbkopf and his friends and acquaintances to think I'm one of those money-grubbing Jews – I don't want to imagine them and their friends saying, "you see, all *they* care about is money. Not the pure and innocent joy of nostalgia, of rediscovery of a former family landmark – no, right away, those grasping, demanding, self-righteous Jews!"

My mood can best be described as both confident and apprehensive. Who wouldn't be apprehensive about meeting the people who laid claim to their property – and even their name – under cover fabricated by the Nazis?

My mood can be best described as vacillating between anger and sadness.

The closer we get to Ansbach, the more I feel like an avenging Michael Kohlhaas, the anodyne, middle-class provincial who, provoked by mistreatment at the hands of an arrogant German margrave, leads a small army of discontented rabble in a doomed uprising against the tyrannical powers that were.

Kohlhaas would have certainly empathized with my anger, which grows as I chew over the words from Kalbkopf's secretary: "he also lives in the house."

"Please slow down," Laura says quietly, as the Volvo jumps forward. The tin box holding my mother's ashes skids across the cargo space.

Eyes fixed on the road ahead, I'm not fully aware that this journey will turn out to be about more than just finding a factory, or discovering new information about my family and their travails; that it's about discovering the true genesis of my fury, and the means by which I might eventually come to terms with it.

2

YOU DO THIS ALL THE TIME

Months earlier, on a Friday afternoon, I am trying to get to the Yankees game, only Max is running around the house naked, screaming. I suppose I should lend a hand in some way.

What happened is that Maddie slipped out the garage door while I was lugging our four-million-ton Sony TV from the Agnostic Era out to the curb, and Maddie will only come to Laura (and then, only if Laura has treats), because Maddie is a cat. Laura is outside, a box of cat treats in her hands, and Max is not happy because he's inside while all the action is taking place outside.

He wants to help, but the way I see it, Max is only making things worse; Maddie is unlikely to find his screaming and tail-and-whisker-grasping an attractive alternative to the great outdoors.

This isn't the first time something like this has happened, and I know Laura worries about coyotes, cars, and the giant hawks that circle our 2 acres of property looking for edible quadrupeds. This time, Maddie has disappeared behind some bushes, and might be headed to the barn across the road.

"I want to help mommy!" Max screams, again.

The clock is ticking on my chances of getting out the door in time to catch my train to Yankee Stadium. There's just one thing to do.

"YOU HAVE TO GROW THE FUCK UP AND SIT DOWN AND LISTEN," I scream at my hyperventilating, refractory three-year-old.

Laura brushes past me as she rushes back inside, her arm trembling so violently you can hear the treats jiggling in the box she's still holding. Her reddish blonde hair is pulled back in a ponytail, her blue eyes piercing cold.

"Have you totally lost your mind?" she asks, her voice low. Her dislike for me has been growing for months.

Max is now sitting, staring up at us from the wooden living room floor, awash in sorrow and confusion. He reminds me of myself some 50 years ago, also sitting on a living room floor looking up at my own parents and crying for forgiveness. I was probably a little older than Max is now, maybe eight or nine years old, but still a kid. It seems like we go through life perpetuating the same spectacles for our children that our parents acted out for us.

I had just confessed to some stupid misdemeanor – stealing money from my father and Valiums from my mother so I could give them to my older sister Bette because she was broke and helpless and I was her knight in shitting pants. My mother was running around the house wailing in a high-pitched voice that she was going to kill my sister for turning me into a delinquent. My 19th-century father ratcheted himself to his feet and from his six-foot height pointed down at me, shouting, ostensibly to my mother, but into my face, "look what you are doing to your son!"

His finger had trembled like Laura's voice is trembling now, like Max's lower tip is trembling, like I'm trembling. Max isn't really sure who is doing what to whom but he has the guts to repeat, this time at a lower volume, "I want to help mommy."

It's times like this when I am overwhelmed with self-pity and all I want to do is cry.

Laura says, "Go, just go. I know you want to go to the game, just go."

"Are you sure?" I say with all the grace of a cover-your-ass spineless slimeball.

The image of Max sitting and crying on the floor stays with me as I'm driving to the Croton-Harmon train station, about 20 minutes away. I think about myself as a little kid living alone in a house with two decidedly ancient parents. My mother was 39 when I was born. My father 59. My five half brothers and sisters had either scrammed or been forced out of the house by the time I was six, making me an only child in fact if not in principle.

I remember my sister Bette saying bitterly that my father should have never had had me at his age. She had said this out of love. He was absent from the usual Little League games, elementary school plays, and Boy Scout Father-Son excursions. Then he died.

I was 55 when Max was born. Again, the same spectacle.

The roads are narrow, with lots of switchbacks, and I swerve to avoid hitting a squirrel. My tires spin momentarily on the driveway gravel of a house with a TRUMP sign on the mailbox. I cross a bridge over the Croton reservoir that sends drinking water to New York City, its quiet surface refracting the late afternoon sunlight into my eyes.

The crowded train is raucous with thick men from even further north, swathed in Budweiser sweat, confidently bantering in anticipation of the whupping the Yanks are about to put on their hapless opponent. I try not to stare at the young women wearing pink Yankee hats and distressed jeans. I have a book, but I can't focus enough to read. I wonder whether Laura has managed to coax Maddie back to the house, and if Max is having his bath, and whether I'm in hot water myself, or something worse.

At the Stadium, I grab a sausage and get to my seat in the upper deck, a Friday night tradition from when I used to come with my daughter Clara before she moved to Colorado. I've kept both seats and can't wait for Max to be old enough to come.

During the middle innings of the game, the Yanks are down a run but they have runners on base. The crowd is roaring. I get a text from Laura: *Maddie is back in the house, whew.*

Whew, I reply quickly, perfunctorily.

I know I should say more, something like 'I'm sorry I let her escape, glad you got her back in the house. Is Max behaving? Sorry about my outburst.'

But you can't text and cheer.

When the Yanks plate their go-ahead run, I turn to high-five a guy standing behind me, the guy who'd spent most of the game explaining the rules of baseball to some friend from elsewhere. I am attuned to elsewhere because, for many years, I too lived elsewhere: in France, where I kept in touch with my inner American child by teaching French kids to play baseball. I think maybe this guy and I can become friends.

The guy high-fives me back and then turns back to his friend from elsewhere. I realize I'm too old to make new friends that easily; that I've got the friends I've got, and the family I've got, as far as that goes.

It's a fractured family.

I once told my boss about needing to give my sister Bette a monthly allowance because she's retired and her social security check is too tiny to keep her afloat, even though she lives in Buttfuck, North Carolina.

"I didn't know you have a sister," my boss responded.

"Yeah, actually I have two sisters and two brothers. And another brother, who died."

"You've never mentioned them," she said, her eyebrows raised.

"They're half-brothers and sisters," I said, then immediately regretted the implication: that they're less to me because they're half-siblings. But there's something to that, too. My parents made them less to me by keeping us apart.

"I never even met my two brothers. I don't even know if they're alive. I just know that the third one isn't."

"Ah," she said, her facial expression as neutral as she could manage.

Of course, I've become accustomed to having siblings I barely know. It's only when I have to tell other people that I'm reminded of just how unusual it is. To have never once, for instance, spoken to my brothers Chris and Johnnie. To have seen my sister Paulette no more than three or four times in my adult life because she was thrown out

8

of the house by my father (19th century!) when she was 17 and pregnant, and moved out to California.

Walter, the half-brother from my father's side, died when I was in my twenties, and we barely knew each other, even though he only lived across the East River in Manhattan. He was an artist, which from my parents' point of view was commendable, but he was gay, which was okay so far as it went, but not a good example for the child (me). So our interactions were limited and usually supervised. My mother explained that homosexuals called themselves gay, but really they were sad because they were destined to live out their lives alone.

Walter never forgave me for having her for a mother.

The Yanks win. The train ride home is loud with bragging, razzing, hazing fans. Their sense of entitlement – that the Yanks will always win, should always win – aggravates me. I love the Yankees, but I understand that winning championships isn't actually a birthright.

Even before Max was born, Laura stopped coming to the games because of the fans. They were too loud and boorish and drunk.

On the way home from the train station, I drive slowly through the dimly lit, twisting roads, careful but also reluctant to face Laura. I know I'm going to hear it again about my temper.

The first time she'd seen me lose my temper, we were on a road trip together, driving down south to see her parents at their South Carolina retirement community. We had twice stopped overnight along the way, sharing in the experience of eating bad Southern food and listening to local radio stations. Laura was brought up in Upstate New York, and she still had some of that farm-girl frankness. But New York City is where she had grown into womanhood, and that combination of Manhattan sophistication and country-girl earthiness had turned me on. We were both old enough to know what we wanted – finally, in my case, after much trial and error – and we knew we had found each other.

We danced in a bar in Charlotte, ignoring the stares from strangers. Laura had trained as a dancer, and it showed, whereas my arthritic ankle, fractured in a baseball game years before, only added to my innate stiffness.

Once we got there, I grew frustrated by the way her parents infantilized her, and by the way she dimmed her lights for them. I didn't feel like I could tell her, though, and my anger began to build. So on the drive back to the city, I picked a fight with her about something else, something insignificant – her parents' decision to play golf in the morning instead of having breakfast with us before we left, or the way her father wore his turtleneck – it doesn't matter.

I pulled over on the side of the road and banged my fist against the steering wheel. I saw the startled look on her face; we had been dating for just a few months but were already engaged, and I could tell she was reconsidering who I was, and to whom she was hitching her wagon.

"I'm sorry," I said quickly. "I just snapped."

"Thank you for saying that," she said, her voice quivering slightly, like the flutter of a cardinal's wings. She factored in the new information, and I saw the resolve form on her face.

"You can't do that. I don't deserve that," she said. "I love you, but I won't live that way."

"I know," I said. I cried, genuine tears of remorse. Not this again, I thought. She put her hand over mind, the one still gripping the steering wheel, white knuckled with shame.

"It's okay," she whispered gently. She leaned across the arm rest and kissed me on the mouth.

When I get to the house late in the suburban night, Laura is waiting. Her back is to me as I walk into the kitchen, and she turns quietly and looks at me with narrowed eyes. She reproaches me for yelling at Max and for failing to apologize for my role in the great cat escape of 2019. We're standing in the kitchen, she a full foot shorter than me, pale skin freckled with light orange starbursts. Tall and stooping, trying to give her space, I try to gauge the seriousness of this conflict – her lips, usually full and smiling, are compressed.

"You do this all the time. The yelling, slapping your hand on the table. All the time," she says.

I *am* sorry about Maddie, but I don't think I'm wholly to blame. How was I supposed to close the basement door while I was struggling with the TV set?

About Max, what could I say? So I say nothing. Instead, I try forcing myself to cry, the self-pity machine in full swing.

Because I realize that I've done it again. I've managed the seemingly impossible, although it's taken me six years of marriage. Laura, who loves me like no other, doesn't like me anymore. I can't blame her.

"I'm sorry," I mumble, hoping for more than forgiveness. Hoping for a do-over, not just about Maddie or Max, but the whole thing, my bad temper, my impatience, my insistence that everything be forgiven me. I want to undo the years of destructive behavior I have inflicted upon her. And I also want Laura to love me unconditionally, to accept and even adore my destructive behaviors. I am trapped in a vicious cycle of my own making. You have to love me the way I expect to be loved, no divergence allowed.

I want to punish myself – to atone, but also to elicit Laura's sympathy. I remember what my father would say to me whenever I complained about being sent to my room: "*My* father would have slapped you."

I consider slapping myself.

I repeat the same shibboleth to myself whenever I've done something intolerably stupid: stubbing my toe on the coffee table, closing the car door on my hand, losing my temper and yelling at my beautiful, loving wife for no good reason. It's like my father is in my ear, reminding me that whatever I've done is so unforgivably stupid that if he had done anything remotely like it, his father would have slapped him.

The original, *echt,* "my father" was my father's stern, unforgiving Prussian father, Hugo Hirschkind, a butcher by trade and a dolt whose Kaiser's bronze star for bravery earned during the war of 1870 hung on a wall in the house in Ansbach where my father grew up. The valorous and handsome son of a butcher who married the heiress to the silk fortune of Bavaria, Hugo Hirschkind would have slapped the shit out of me for messing up what it shouldn't have been possible to mess up.

He would have slapped me for taking a smitten young woman and turning her into something she isn't: a scold, carping at her infantile husband as if he were a child, rather than the tall, blue eyed man she'd married, with a full head of dark hair and the ability, even in his 50s, to smack line drives in the batting cage.

She had not married this: a grown man leaning against the kitchen counter, willing himself to cry in the hopes that his wife would forgive him everything, like his mother forgave him everything. Despairing of hearing Laura ever refer to him again as "my handsome husband."

Now, she says, "I don't know if I can go on like this much longer. I really don't."

One evening during the last cold, long-ass winter – before having screamed at Max for being a little boy wanting to help his mommy chase down a pet cat – I am in the plush rocking chair in his bedroom, Max cradled in my arms, dropping off to sleep to the sound of my voice.

So, Milo was a little boy who lived a long time ago, before there were airplanes or cars or machines of any kind. And he lived with his mommy and daddy in a house in a village next to the ocean, and every night, he would go out and watch the waves come in. And he would wonder, do the waves bring more starfish to shore when they come in, or take away more starfish as they go out?

With my free hand, I mimic the movement of the waves crashing down and then pulling back, speaking slow and rhythmic like my heart, like his heart, my little Max. Max has his Milo stories, just as Thurman had his Julien stories and my daughter Clara had her Tina stories. All of the stories inspired by the Hero's Journey, each of them one of a thousand faces.

Max is still too young for Milo to battle monsters, so for now his secret power is his ability to speak to the animals.

Milo saw his friends Peter Rabbit and Mr. Snodgrass, the porcupine, and Mr. Snodgrass peed, and Peter Rabbit sniffed the pee and laughed.

What's so funny? Milo asked.

Mr. Snodgrass just told me a joke. You should sniff it, said Peter.

So Milo bent down and sniffed it and he started to laugh.

What was the joke? Max asks, sleepily.

"I'm getting to that," I say.

The pee said: I saw Mr. Bear and I said, are you Winnie the Poop?

Max laughs.

Like my father, I have two sons by two different women, more than two decades apart. Thurman is now almost 25, while his half-brother Max is three. They've met each other exactly twice. And then, to trump my father, I have a daughter by still yet another woman, Liz. Clara is 23, and also hasn't seen much of Max because she lives in Colorado.

I had Thurman in France, with a French woman who now loathes me. I moved back to the United States without him, when he was 10, and my parenting opportunities with Thurman became limited to annual summer visits and weekly Skype calls. I sometimes remembered to get Clara on our calls as well – but rarely.

At an age when many boys are bonding with their actual fathers over sports, Thurman was seeking father figures from among the fathers of friends on the soccer fields of Paris.

Try explaining to an 11-year-old, over the course of a Skype call, how the dinosaurs became extinct.

Now at least with Max, I don't have to struggle. I Google a YouTube video, and there's a handful of computer-generated reenactments of meteor strikes and fireballs.

Here Max, this is what an extinction event looks like.

3

THE DOG OF ONE SUMMER

The world has been ending since the beginning. The Garden of Eden. The Flood. The Tower of Babel. It goes on and on. One thing after another, an asteroid, a volcanic eruption, a solar flare. Extinction event after extinction event, and yet we go on. The First Temple, the Second Temple, the plague, the Great War, the War to End all Wars, the Bomb; acts of God, acts of Nature, acts of Man – it doesn't matter, we build again.

My boss calls. She's our company's head of global communications. She is a former lawyer, in her forties, with lustrous black hair and a severe smile. A firm believer that looks confer power, she keeps herself skinny by limiting her lunch and dinner intake to two hard boiled eggs. She speaks just as economically. Like me, she works from her home office, only going into the office to confer with senior executives.

"Hickins," she says. For some reason, everyone at the company calls me by my last name. "People are freaking out about that *Times* article. Can you help?"

By "people," she means our CEO and a couple of EVPs. One of my jobs – what she calls my superpower – is finding journalistic flaws in articles about our company that these higher-ups don't like, and using my knowledge of editorial process to exact corrections (and sometimes a retraction). Flaws such as, you didn't include our statement high enough in the story, or completely enough, or you misconstrued such and such a time-line. Sometimes the flaws were germane, and at other times they were mere technicalities.

But when you're dealing with scrupulous editors, a mistake is a mistake is a mistake, and must be corrected on the record. We then use the fact that a story was corrected to discredit it in its entirety.

It's the most exciting part of my job.

Let me restate that: it's the only exciting part of my job. But job satisfaction isn't high on my current list of priorities. I had that once, when I was a journalist, but it didn't pay well enough.

I prioritize reading the offending article over finalizing a press release, and am just getting started when Laura knocks on the door to my office. (Laura also works from home, but she doesn't have an office. This is one of the million ways Laura bends over backwards for me.)

"Your mother says she has another belly ache," Laura says through the door.

"Michou," my mother says. "I'm feeling very bad. I have a *böse* pain in my stomach. I think we should call the ambulance."

For the millionth time, probably literally. And that's only for the 90 days since she's been living here at our house.

"Okay," I say peevishly. "Fine."

She shuffles into my office and sits heavily in my desk chair and winces. I notice her pink scalp through her thinning white hair. She isn't wearing her dentures, making her mouth soft and vulnerable looking. I pick up my phone and watch her sink into the brown leather swivel chair and exhale. Her head is thrown back slightly, her mouth agape, and I watch expectantly for her next movement as I dial 911. There isn't one. An arm is resting on the arm of the chair, the other across her belly.

"Mom," I say. "*Maman. Reponds-moi, maman.*" Answer me.

She's still breathing, but deeply unconscious. She could be sleeping. I have never seen anyone do that before.

"Hello," I say when the 911-operator answers the call. I steady my voice, which I find is fracturing. "Yes, hi, my mother has just collapsed. I think she's dead – dying or dead, I'm not sure."

Laura is already crying. For once, my mother is right. She needs an ambulance. It's a running joke among Jewish sons and their mothers. Among Jewish sons and their siblings: for once, she was right.

"If anyone was ready, it was her," I say to the paramedics.

She had prepared for it meticulously: the DNR, the living will, the constant reminders to open the metal box ("the key is hidden in my middle desk drawer. Don't forget the metal box.")

Laura hands me the DNR and the living will, both of which we keep in the kitchen junk drawer – also at my mother's insistence.

"I'll walk Junie and follow you in the car," Laura says.

I sit in front with the driver as the ambulance weaves through traffic. "Hold on tight. People always try to beat the ambulance to the spot." Time and again he slams on the brakes, punches the horn like it's a face.

At the hospital, I hand the doctor my mother's paperwork. He's too young to be a doctor. It's almost as if he's glued stubble to his face. He reminds me of Wooly Willy, the toy where you use a small magnet to drag iron filings that look like razor stubble across a cardboard clown face.

Laura finally arrives.

"We could operate," says Wooly Willy. "But it might not save her life. If it did, it would only prolong her life for a few hours or days, and it wouldn't be a very comfortable life."

I point to the living will he's still holding.

"I'll let you and your wife think about it," he says.

There's nothing to think about. It's been all thought through, for once. I point again to the DNR.

"I'll wait over here," he says.

"There's nothing to think about," I say.

"I'll be over there. There's no rush."

I am apparently failing as a child. I'm supposed to be distraught, beside myself, besotted with grief, grief-struck, grief-stricken, struck mute, stuck, stymied, stuttering with grief and desolation.

I'm none of those things. I'm the original boy who didn't cry at his father's funeral. I'm the repressed bastard all these wives, lovers and children have complained about for years. After everything she endured, after everything my father endured – revolution, wars, hunger, huge personal loss – and I can't even squeeze out a single tear, not even a fake one.

I ask Laura for the eye drops she uses for her contact lenses. I squeeze a few drops into the corner of my eye and wait for them to run down my cheek. I go back to the doctor and solemnly tell him we've decided to let her have a quiet, dignified death.

Wooly Willy puts a hand on my shoulder. "I know this is hard," he says.

No, I think.

"It's hard to bury a parent," he says.

"We're not burying her. She's an atheist. She wants to be cremated."

They wheel her into a room meant for dying, and Laura and I follow. Technically, my mother is still alive.

"Talk to her," Laura says.

"She can't hear me."

"You never know."

"It doesn't mean anything," I say.

"You don't know that."

Laura is more spiritual than I am.

"You should call your sister," she says. She means Bette, the one who still talks to our mother.

"Yeah," I say.

I sit next to my mother's bed, trying to think of something to say. Hey mom, it'll be okay.

No, that's what I said to my father the last time I saw him, and he snorted and said, "Sure," that sarcastic motherfucker.

Try something else. Hey mom, I spoke to Bette last week. I guess I'll call her later and tell her you're dead.

No, that doesn't sound very positive.

Her life: a fat, sick, old woman, widowed at 54, when that was considered hideously old, never again to love a man after a lifetime of living the lust for life as faithfully as one of Iggy Pop's stooges; angry, middle class and highbrow, arrogant, limousine liberal, aloof and disdainful of the "masses" on whose behalf she fustigated in the privacy of her wood-burning-stove-warmed cabin in the woods, far from the maddening people whose company she couldn't stand. "I have compassion for almost all the individuals in the world," she once said, channeling Charles Bukowski. "But people repulse me."

These last couple of months have given me the gift of rediscovering her as a mother but also as a woman with a past. Whose story revealed itself slowly, begrudgingly, of men betrayed, of bitter strife, children abandoned, forgiveness craved if never asked.

Then my mother takes a last, long, noisy breath and stops in mid-exhale.

"Bye. Mom," I say, my voice barely above a whisper.

I don't dare touch her. I ring for the nurse.

Her mouth is still open, her eyes closed – almost as if squinting into an uncertain distance. The expression on her face is fearful, desperate, and greedy for one last gasp. The former stage actress was never more beautiful, nor more fearsome. She was finally the Bette Davis she always wanted to be.

"I think she's gone," I say.

The nurse, in her fifties, pale white with blue eyes, confirms this.

"I'm sorry, son. My condolences," she says with a hint of Irish accent.

"Well," I say, "it was a good death after all. She died at home with her family around her, she wasn't alone."

The nurse looks at me like I'm from another planet.

Aren't we supposed to be strong at moments like this?

My older brother Walter made a spectacle of himself at our father's funeral, throwing himself on the pile of dirt next to the grave and trying to throw fistfuls of it onto the pine coffin where my father's body was already decomposing.

The old men from the temple with the tattoos on their forearms held him back as best they could, shushing him and remonstrating in their thick German and Polish accents.

I didn't cry then and I don't intend to cry now.

I hadn't cried for my father because losing my father, losing everything I hated, was too immense of a loss to comprehend. How would I know what I didn't want to become if I didn't have his furious example in front of me? How could I know he would bequeath me a lifetime of barely repressed fury, or why he carried it with him?

Death was probably a relief for him, and it was certainly a relief for me to have that crabby, sickly, pain-ridden old fucker out of my 15-year-old life. Still, I hated myself for not crying at his funeral, for not being able to summon up some kind of croak or even a sob.

I don't intend to cry now either, because my mother's death is as good a death as anyone has any right to expect. She placed two sons in foster care, openly despised her two daughters, and clung so desperately to me, her one remaining, last-born offspring, that I pushed her away for a long as I could. Why should I spoil her good death by crying over her body? That carcass had betrayed her for too long anyhow with its aches and pains.

Laura and I get some food at the diner across the street from the funeral parlor where they'll cremate her remains.

I find myself tearing up. "I don't know why I'm crying," I say.

Laura puts a soft hand on mine. "It's a natural reaction," she says. She clearly can't believe she has to say this.

"Natural for who?" I say.

She pulls her hand away.

I pick up my mother's ashes a few months later, while on my way back from buying some printer toner and a ream of paper at Staples. I keep the ashes in her prized tin red-and-black box of Swee-Touch-Nee Tea, sealed as hermetically as a tea tin can be. I make a mental note to suggest this as a new jingle for the tea company.

We don't have a ceremony of any kind. We know she's dead, and anyway, who would we invite?

Laura lets me keep the box on the mantle in the living room, although sometimes I find it back in my office, between the printer and the PC screen.

A few weeks after her death, we drive up to my mother's cabin, and we start going through her stuff. I'm going to sell the cabin for whatever I can get – it's an insulated piece of crap with a wood stove, an illegal septic, a temperamental well, and mouse droppings on every surface, sitting on five acres of marshland.

Her furniture is worn down and pullulating with insects. The pages of the books on her shelves have been eaten by the mice she refused to kill. The fan on her computer is jammed by a mouse nest. Newspaper clippings are piled on the floor – lawsuits by local Native Americans against the county, the local police blotter, a story about new archeological discoveries in Crete that could originate with the Trojan War, and a letter she wrote that was published in the Stamford Gazette:

Dear Editor:

People die every day. Tragedy touches every human life. But those of us who love our animal companions will understand why I have to say a few words about The Dog of One Summer.

It happens that we meet an individual who impacts our life with an unexpected strength. Our contact may be brief or not, time has little to do with it. For me that individual was a young Black Lab named Mitzie, who came into my life last July, and was killed three months later in a stupid road accident.

I have been fortunate enough to have known several canine persons in the course of my life, but being old, I have necessarily outlived them all. This time, I thought I would not have to face that pain, and it was good to imagine that after I die my family would give the sweet dog a happy home. Alas! It was not to be. Within the time it takes to draw a breath, her life was snatched from her, and a gaping, aching hole was left in my heart. I shall always miss her, my Mitzie.

Viviane Hickins, South Gilboa, New York

. . .

I remember that letter because she sent a copy of it around to all of us – prompting a call from my sister Bette complaining that she had never cared for any of her own kids as much (except for me, of course).

My mother had saved a bunch of other files and old crap in a locked metal box, the key to which was right where she told me, and reminded me with every visit – in the desk drawer. I flip through the folders quickly, not expecting to find anything significant, and am rewarded by not finding anything of significance. I see that it contains official papers – her certificate of naturalization, a college transcript from France, and the divorce decree from her first husband, Juan Antonio. I don't look any further, and I close the box.

Our olfactory senses are overwhelmed with the odor of decay.

"What's that smell?" Laura asks.

"Mouse droppings," I say.

Amidst the other mess I find a small wooden box that closes with a latch. It's my father's sample case from when he used to travel on behalf of the Kupfer silk thread manufacturing company, founded by his maternal grandfather, Edward Kupfer. The box is made of cherry wood, with varnish applied so thoroughly that it still shines a hundred years after it was made. Inside are bobbins of silk thread in 26 different varieties of color and weight. My mother in recent years used the thread to darn her clothes, so the bobbins are somewhat askew and the threads are tangled up. I sigh at the disarray.

Laura misunderstands. "Do you want to postpone the reading?" she asks. I am due to give a reading at our local bookstore after we drive back home this afternoon. My new e-book, *I Lived in France and So Can You,* has just been released. I regret my mother missed seeing it get published, because it's in some way an homage to her influence on my life. I never would have lived in France had it not been for her background.

I call Clara, the 23-year-old I had with Liz, to tell her about the cabin. To ask if she minds if I sell it and split up the proceeds among us – she, Bette, Paulette, and Thurman.

"Do whatever you want. You always do anyway," she says. And she's not finished with me.

"You know, I've been thinking about the history of your family, and the war and all, and it kind of makes sense that it seems natural to you to have a bunch of family scattered all over the fucking place. It makes it easier to forgive you," she adds.

I'm not sure what forgiveness means in this case. Is it a blanket amnesty, or is it limited to a specific offense? It seems like I can't ever get truly clear of recriminations from either Clara or Thurman.

"What the hell are you talking about?" I say. "I can't control where my sister lives, or that my brothers disappeared before I ever knew them."

"Yeah, but look at you, your own family. Or what there is of it. One son is in France, I'm in fucking Boulder, mom's in Manhattan, and you and your new family are up in the Hudson Valley somewhere. None of us know each other, none of us have had a chance to know each other. How many times have I even seen Max. Forget about Thurman – you never even tried."

Her voice cracks.

I inherited a fractured family and have mostly done a good job of perpetuating a softer version of the same tendencies, as if repeating history were a unique business opportunity I received in an email from a destitute Nigerian prince.

4

FAMILY-OWNED FOR MORE THAN 135 YEARS

An email comes into my work inbox from someone named Luis Castillo. It's late afternoon, and I'm inclined to ignore it until morning. But the subject line catches my eye: *Viviane Bronstein Castillo Hickins was my grandmother.*

Viviane Bronstein Castillo Hickins was *my mother.* Which would make this guy my... nephew?

I read the subject line a second and third time, before even opening the email itself.

Luis Castillo, are you some elaborate bot machine? A crank or a grifter or a psychopath?

I take a breath and open the email. It reads:

Are we related? I don't want anything from you. I want to know my story... never knew my father, who was perhaps your older half-brother, John Fredrick Castillo.

I lean back in my Staples desk chair. John Frederick Castillo, aka Johnnie. Father to this Luis, previously unknown to all – or so I believed.

I am a little surprised to be hearing from a long-lost nephew at this stage of my life. I have spent a number of fruitless hours over the years looking for relatives, poring over Facebook profiles and the vast

Internet of People, and I have by this point figured they simply don't exist.

There is something about the plain-spoken directness of his language that makes me trust him intrinsically. Unlike my work friend who sardonically asks, "How long until he asked you for money?"

I write back: *Wow, yes, I guess we are related. I'd love to talk and 'catch up,' so to speak. Where are you based?*

Hawaii, it turns out.

He sends me his number and we immediately get on FaceTime. I do a little quick math. Johnnie was 19 years older than me, so this nephew could be about my age. He's leanly muscled, with high cheekbones and shoulder length hair tied off in a ponytail. His eyes seem to squint permanently to ward off the effects of the sun, and his face is wrinkled and a little leathery. He gives off a simple vibe, like someone uncomplicated by the bullshit of guile, but he's also smart. He lives on an organic farm he runs with his interior-decorator wife Karen and an older son from a first marriage. He has three other children with Karen, all girls.

He wants to travel now that his girls are all out of the house. He thinks he may have some Spanish blood because of his last name – Castillo – which has led him to various DNA websites, and now to me. He saw the obituary I had published for my mother, connected me to my LinkedIn page, and thus addressed a note to my professional email address.

"My mother didn't want me to know my father, and that was good enough for me. She was the wisest person I knew, and her word was gold. But now I realize, I've never even seen a picture of him," he says.

It's lucky for him I didn't throw away half the stuff from my mother's cabin – lucky I listened to Laura when she told me that even if I didn't have the inclination to look through that old junk, one of my kids might want to one day.

24

After I hang up with Luis, I head for the basement to hunt for my mother's metal box. It's a heavy-duty, fire-resistant gray steel box made to hold around 50 standard manila folders.

I switch on the overhead light, a solidary lightbulb hanging from the ceiling. Our basement is bare bones concrete, the walls lined with metal shelves holding dozens of plastic storage boxes. Each box is labeled "Laura keepsakes" or "Michael papers" or "Clothes."

Down there is where we also have Laura's stationary bicycle, an elliptical machine I never use anymore, a few mismatched sets of free weights, a few plastic folding chairs for when we have guests, and a stretching table. It's a cluttered mess with some organizational effort thrown in.

I find my mother's metal box and open it with the key I left in the lock so I don't lose it.

It contains around 30 folders, which at first glance contain photographs and official records, like marriage, birth and death certificates, a few report cards – in other words, the typical paper trail of our lives. Some documents have been jammed between folders, or have slipped to the bottom of the box. I look for a photograph of my half-brother Johnnie, Luis's long-lost father.

"Dinner's going to be ready in an hour," Laura shouts down from the top of the stairs.

"Spectacular," I say, intentionally jaunty and over-the-top.

"What does that mean?" Laura asks.

"It means great. No problem, perfect, thank you."

It doesn't take long for me to find a folder with a trove of loose photos, including one taken of my two older brothers when they were kids. It's undated, black and white, probably from the early 1950s.

It's obviously winter, and they're both wearing wool aviator-style hats with ear flaps.

On the back, in my mother's handwriting: "Chris and Johnnie, 103rd street playground."

They're easy to tell apart. Chris is the older one, smiling at the camera, while Johnnie is skinny and scowling. Even with the disparity in ages, his resemblance to Luis is amazing.

There's another. A Christmas photo from 1952, my mother's four kids together for maybe the last time before the boys get sent to foster families. This was before she met my father. A tree with trimmings in the living room of an improbable Jewish-American household consisting of Russian and Mexican refugees spanning three generations, each deeply suspicious of the others, a couple of gifts on the floor under the branches, joy and tension reflected in their little kid poses – 12-year-old Chris trying to look adult and serious, 10-year-old Johnnie mugging for the camera and pretending to punch an invisible foe, eight-year old Bette smiling and hoping someone notices, six-year old Paulette staring straight ahead expressionlessly. My mother's mother sitting in a stiff wooden chair, looking sad, probably disapproving of the non-Jewish Christmas tree. I wasn't there yet, of course – I wouldn't be born for nine more years.

I find other stuff in the box: a picture of a tough looking kid (Johnnie) on a laminated US immigration card, taken when he was seven. A couple of his junior high school report cards, and a form letter with the name and address of Johnnie's foster parents. A letter from the Navy explaining the conditions of Johnnie's arrest for desertion and subsequent and unusual discharge – a seemingly made-up-on-the-spot category – "for mental instability."

There didn't seem to be a reason why my mother kept some of these mementos and not others.

She kept a letter, dated February 18, 1971, from a woman named Linda Jones. Johnnie would have been 28 years old. Linda, it turns out, was Luis's wise mother.

Dear Viviane,

I am very ashamed to have delayed writing this letter for so long but at last – on July 22, 1970, a baby son, Luis Christopher was born. He is a truly beautiful child and is already learning to crawl, sit up, and to walk in his walker. He has sandy curly hair and gray blue eyes at the moment.

I have seen Johnnie only once since Luis was born. He came over to see

*little Luis and I just asked him to go away. I feel very sorry for him and love
him still, but the only way we could be together is if there were no children
involved. He is much the same now as when we met, and is still associated
with drugs.*

The letter proves on thing for sure: my mother knew about Luis. It
makes me wonder why she didn't tell me, and what else she hid from
me. It occurs to me that she didn't think I'd care – probably because
she didn't. After all, what was another scrabbling, graspy, needy ego
to her?

I sit down on one of the folding chairs we've relegated to the
basement. I hear Max running and Laura's footsteps on the ceiling
above me, and I'm aware that I'm probably needed upstairs. But I'm
not quite ready to re-emerge.

I was mildly surprised, but not shaken, to discover I have a
nephew. However, realizing my mother knew about him and never
told me is a bit of a shock. It implies there might be other surprises.

The form letter about the foster parents – that's not a surprise
either. It confirms what I'd been told – that my mother put Chris and
Johnnie in foster homes (separate ones, no less) because their
grandmother couldn't cope with raising four little kids while their
mother, her daughter Vivi, went out partying.

The Navy discharge confirms Johnnie's tumultuous relationship
with authority figures, and his general reputation for bad-assery.
Linda's letter confirms his drug use and abuse; and also his charm.

I pick up a picture of my mother, a glamor shot really, probably
taken by a friend who dabbled in photography, that shows her as a
young woman sure of her 1940s Hollywood looks. I can imagine her
flirting in the Manhattan Copacabana nightclub night, coming
home to her mother's apartment on West 113th street when all the
lights are out, free of Juan Antonio Castillo – her supposedly
abusive first husband – tipsy, lighting a cigarette as she crosses the
threshold of the apartment, angry at being saddled with four kids –
two sons too much for her aging mother to handle on her own, two
girls too unlike herself to be any fun. None of this is a surprise to

me, but the photos and other paperwork make it more real than ever before.

There are no photographs of Johnnie as an adult.

Decades-old dust cause me a sudden sneezing fit.

"You okay down there?" Laura calls down.

"Fine," I say between sneezes.

"Dinner's ready."

"I'm coming." I haven't seen the hour go by, and I wonder how much of our lives are spent this way – so engaged with the past that we neglect the present.

Reluctantly, I leave the metal box behind, only dimly aware that it contained even more fragments of my family for me to discover.

After dinner, I email Luis scans of the photographs and send him the originals by regular mail. After all, they're his.

Luis emails me a few days later, and the connection has clearly moved him.

Hi Michael,

I can't thank you enough for those documents, and especially the pictures. The first time I've seen my father's image. I can't wait to get into Viviane's family history. It's crazy, yesterday I'm driving around trying to do my work with my eyes full of tears, (of joy), and I'm not sure why, just gratitude, I think. And I'm someone that all three of my daughters say they have almost never seen cry. Just want you to know the depth of the impact that our meeting has on my life. Thank you for opening up to me.

He wants a relationship, he wants to be in my life. That in itself is a novelty. Our family has no track record of sticking together.

Luis sends me photos of his family. His wife Karen is tall and slender, with high cheekbones, beautiful lips. Easy to fall in love with, a glint in her eyes and a knowing smile for the photographer.

He has two grandkids from his eldest son, Bruce – two little boys standing at surf's edge, long hair and glistening with droplets of sea water, looking like baby gods of the deep.

Later that night, I'm in my home office, toking on a bowl of weed in an elephant-shaped ceramic pipe Laura and I bought while on our honeymoon in Jamaica. Better days. We met while I was still at *The Wall Street Journal* and she was a well-established public relations executive. We had drinks to talk about some of her clients. Then dinner. There was a jauntiness to her. A few weeks later, a Yankees game.

"This isn't a date," she said. "You're married, and I don't date married men."

By then, Liz and I were just waiting for Clara to go off to college before going our separate ways. But Laura wasn't buying it – she smiled at me, expressing something between complicity, amusement, and equanimity that I found irresistible.

A second Yankees game, drinks at a bar near her place, a clumsy avowal: "I've got a pretty serious crush on you," I said.

"Aw," she said and smiled. That was it, that was all she would give me.

I set up a meeting between her and Liz, so Liz could vouch for me. Later, Liz gave me her verdict: "she's adorable."

Laura and I started dating, making out like teenagers in local bars. Her lips were smooth and toned, and her smile was graced by a rebellious tooth that coquettishly turned its sharp edge to the world. I could sense her vulnerability; never married to this point, no kids, and resigned to never having any. I checked in with myself: are you serious about her, or is it just the breasts, her narrow waist, and her jauntiness? Do not fuck with her feelings.

I'm serious about her, I reassured myself, as if talking to my father, or asking for her father's blessing.

I leaned into her and she inhaled my aftershave. "I love that cologne," she said. "It's the same my father wears."

She teased me because my favorite music is the Beatles. I told her she was keeping me young by playing me pop tunes on the car radio.

When we went on our honeymoon, she booked us a couple's massage, and I didn't have the heart to tell her I hate massages. I particularly hate anyone touching my hamstrings, or the back of my knees.

"You seem so tense," she said, touching me lightly as we sat in the waiting area in our white cotton robes and underwear.

"I've never had this kind of massage before," I said.

"You're kidding? Didn't any of your other wives know how to treat you?" she laughed.

"This is good. You're forcing me to challenge myself," I said.

"This isn't supposed to be a challenge." She laughed again.

I wonder if I'll ever hear that laugh again. I wonder why I'm so moved by the sudden appearance of Luis Castillo in my life. Is it the product of some mid-life nostalgia for relationships I've lost through death or distraction?

I flip through the folder that holds the papers I found for Luis, and notice one I hadn't seen before. It is a stiff, yellowed business card belonging to a certain Paul Kupfer.

Paul Kupfer apparently immigrated to the United States long before the war. The business card lists a Union Square address.

My boss calls despite the hour. She wants to know when I'm planning to finish the byline I'm ghostwriting for Mr. Bigshot, our CEO.

"The deadline is coming up, and the piece still has to go through legal," she says.

"I'm working on it now." I keep fingering Paul Kupfer's business card. I didn't know there was another Kupfer anywhere in the world, let alone New York.

"I'll have the byline to you in the morning," I say.

"Perfect," she says. She hangs up, talkative as ever.

I get back to pretending to be the billionaire CEO of a company worth hundreds of billions pretending he knows how it feels to be the owner of an Ace Hardware Store franchise, or the director of marketing for a midsized Midwest shoelace manufacturer.

I try to make him sound like a McKinsey wise guy by talking about Schrodinger's cat – a stray named Hobson who cut his paw on Occam's razor, but managed to crawl out through the Overton window. As far as we know, the cat is still alive.

I use lots of tough-guy words, like "vector" and "hot-seat" and "thrive-not-survive." Our CEO actually says things like "sales are inclining" instead of "sales are increasing," probably because he thinks it impresses people with the vastness of his intelligence.

My bile is inclining.

I finish at one a.m. and clump upstairs, then push the dog into the middle of the bed. Max wakes up calling for me at 5:30, and I stagger into his bedroom.

"Is it early?" he asks in the pre-dawn penumbra. He pronounces it "ollie."

"It's super ollie. Will you go back to sleep?"

"I want to eat breakfast," he says.

You can't deprive your kid of sustenance, can you, even as he's depriving you of sleep? It's unconstitutional.

I put another piece of future landfill in the Keurig coffee machine, open a plastic container, theoretically recyclable, and shake a few pieces of pre-cut mango that got here via gallons of fossil fuels onto a plastic plate, put an episode of *Blaze and the Monster Machines* on the on-demand channel, and walk to my office to email the draft to my boss.

My eyes fall again on Paul Kupfer's business card, and I wonder if there's any record of him or his family. I start Googling Kupfer in New York. I get nothing, because there is no such person. I broaden the search to the United States – still nothing. I broaden it further to encompass the universe.

I hit upon this: "Eduard Kupfer Nähseiden Fabrik – Family run for more than 135 years."

It is a silk factory in my father's hometown of Ansbach, and I realize that this is the exact same silk factory my great-grandfather Eduard Kupfer founded in Germany in 1885. The one that my father ran after his own father's death, until the Nazis dispossessed him. The one with the Victorian-style three-story brick house on the grounds where my father Max grew up. In other words, my family's silk factory.

I'm stunned that it's still in existence. But *my* family hasn't been running this place for the last 135 years – we were fucked out of it in 1936 – and that's the only family worth talking about.

This, it sinks in slowly and in powerful waves, is the place where my father grew up, even if he'd never so much as showed me a photograph. But there's the three-story house he once described to me, the color of mocha cream filling. Adjacent to the house is a one-story factory building, all enclosed within a stone wall, with a nice garden out front, a wooden swing hanging off the branch of an ancient oak – it's all right there on the website.

I look for a sign of my father, of my grandfather, or my awkward aunt on her gangly legs, or a mezuzah on a doorpost – or something. Some sign of this family that has run the factory for more than 135 years.

The website doesn't show any actual people. The factory floor is dotted with spindles, steam compressors, dyeing and drying and stirring and shaking machines. The exterior of both buildings are made of stone and wood, with façade ornaments from another time.

I keep coming back to the phrase on the website, "Family run for more than 135 years." As if nothing had happened out of the ordinary. As if my family were still running it, and not some other family that was gifted it through an unspeakable act of evil.

I get off the chair and pace my small office. My father's livelihood was taken from him, yet the business continues to thrive. It makes me angry.

Max cries out to me – the episode of "*Blaze and the Monster Machines*" has ended. Laura is still upstairs in our bedroom. I go back to the kitchen, grab a granola bar for Max and play the next episode. Max once asked me to make the deer we sometimes see grazing outside our windows reappear, and I had to explain that real life isn't on-demand. He didn't seem to fully grasp what I meant, and the more I explained, the less sure I felt of what I was saying.

I retreat to my office, to the spectacle of the Eduard Kupfer Nähseiden Fabrik website and its 135 years of appropriation flashing across my computer screen.

I knew it had been taken over during the war by Reinhold Lutz, my aunt's former husband. But no one ever said the business was still a going concern. It had never even occurred to me to ask anyone about it.

More than George Washington slept here – the factory is like the log cabin Abe Lincoln built with his own two hands before he was born, at least to me.

It's the home of the man who has given me my unwanted mantra, "*my father would have slapped you.*"

Something is at war within me. Part of me understands that this factory has long since passed into the annals of history. There is no recovering anything for me, I don't think.

But part of me feels wronged, and like exacting revenge. Fuck those people who took it from him – from us – and who dare flaunt a family history that doesn't belong to them anymore than the factory should!

Impulsively, I open another tab on my browser and Google "Nazi reparations." I expect to find a website that clearly delineates who is entitled to file a claim and who isn't. But instead I find a tiresome tangle of websites run by a variety of German state and federal governments, NGOs, specialized lawyers, and pressure groups, each explaining convoluted theoretical cases and confusing arrays of filing deadlines – some of them hopelessly in the past, others looming in the next year or so.

It's too exhausting to think about – I have enough to manage without having to deal with lawyers and concomitant paperwork, not to mention my father probably exhausted all the possibilities – or so you would think. And as for the deadlines – I have enough of those already.

I dismiss the possibility. I'm not destitute.

I go back to the kitchen, where Laura is sitting cross-legged on the floor, helping Max with a wooden six-piece puzzle. She's still wearing her deliberately unsexy nightgown, which I nevertheless find titillating in its homespun white cotton plainness.

"We should go there," she says when I tell her what I've found.

"Go where?"

"You want to go to Paris anyway to visit Thurman, right? How far away can it be? We rent a car, we visit the factory. Maybe there's even a way to get something out of it."

"Oh Christ," I say. "Do you have to take over everything, even my own family history?"

She presses her lips together, the sign that I have again offended that god which is her love for me. Another dent in the armor of Eros.

"I'm sorry," I say. "I'm agitated."

"I can see that," she says.

"But also I looked into that already. I'm not sure I'm entitled to anything, the statutes of limitations, there's all kinds of adjudicating bodies. And I don't have the time. I'm pushing 60 years old, this all happened what, 85 years ago, and I don't know."

She gives me a baleful look that says, "I can't believe I have to explain this to you."

"It's not just about you. Have you thought about Max, and Thurman and Clara? It's their history too, their heritage – and the money might mean a lot to them. Max's college..." her voice trails off, hopeless.

She stands up, her long legs strong from carrying Max to the playroom, her calf muscles taut, her skin the creamy white only redheads produce. I want to pull her to me, pull her crotch to my lips, but I know that won't be welcome – not now, not later tonight, or any night soon. We no longer have make-out sex, or make-up sex, or hardly any kind of sex.

I've become embarrassed to tell her how I feel, and I hide my own disappointment, exacerbating the long string of slights both of us nurse like a bottle of soda that's been open too long, gone warm and lost its fizz.

I realize she's right. The money would be good, and the more I think about it, the more the 135-years bit sticks in my craw.

"I can make part of it a business trip and expense my ticket," I say.

I'm also wondering if there's anything new I can learn about my father. I didn't have him for very long, and he never had a chance to talk to me about the facts of life. Let me restate that: he never deemed me mature or worthy enough to tell me about the facts of his life. Whatever happened to him during the war, whatever happened right

34

after the war, whatever caused him to leave his factory behind, whatever happened to his first wife – he barely spoke about any of those things.

All I knew from conversational snippets as rare as fragments of Heraclitus was that the Nazis had killed his beloved mother, and that he would never go back to Germany. And that his father would have slapped me.

Once, when I was still a kid, I was dragged up to the Catskills where I met a Mr. Oscar White at a concentration camp survivors' reunion of two. My father had helped Mr. White obtain a visa to the United States while they were both interned at the St. Cyprien concentration camp in France. I gathered his name had once been Weiss but he Americanized it once he got here.

The adults, mostly relatives of Mr. White's, formed a circle around my father and listened to his every word with rapt attention, while Mr. White's grandchildren wrestled me into a mud pit in the back yard and rubbed my face in the dirt, probably as revenge for having to spend however many hours putting up with stories about my father and how great he was.

How many generations have to be grateful for the actions of a single man? And how annoying to be constantly reminded that you owe your existence to the actions of some geriatric old codger whose visit requires putting on a suit and stiff leather shoes on a Sunday!

———

"So you're saying yes now? A minute ago you had thought it all the way through, and I was an idiot for not following along, and now you've changed your mind?"

"I'm a fast thinker. It's why you married me," I quip. "And I think you're right. I owe it to the kids. Fuck, I owe it to myself. Family-owned for 135 years my ass. Let's see if we can shake some money off that 100-year-old tree."

"Maybe I can visit my Estonian customers," she says. "Unless you want to go alone."

"No way," I say. "I want to share this with you."

A pause.

"Can we go to Prague? You know I've always wanted to go."

Laura was 20 when the Czechs had their Velvet Revolution, and it had become the trendy new travel destination, the homeland of Franz Kafka and Vaclav Havel, the birthplace of Western bohemianism, the fairy tale city reborn from the depredations of Communism.

"Sure. We can do that, after we visit Ansbach."

And I think maybe we'll have 135-year-old sex in honor of our visit.

"To Whom it May Concern: I am Michael Hickins, son of Max Hirschkind and Dora Kupfer, whose family founded your silk factory. I have never been to Germany before and am taking my family on a trip to Europe. Would you allow me to visit your factory and see where my father grew up?"

I am deliberately obsequious and vague. I don't mention that I've spent a dozen years in France, or that one of my children was born and lives in Paris, or that I am suddenly filled with resentment as well as curiosity.

An email comes back the next day:

"Mr. Hickins: Our general manager Mr. Klaus Kalbkopf will most of the month be present in company. He would show you factory, he also lives in the house. To be able to schedule your visit, please let us know what time approximately you will be in the area.

("Signed") Sabine Weber, executive assistant to the general manager."

He also lives in the house! My father's house, and his father's before him.

I buy plane tickets for the three of us, before it occurs to me to see if my daughter Clara wants to come. She lives in Boulder, living her own life, a fragment of the strewn-apart family.

I call her and fill her in on the details of the trip.

"The house? Doesn't she mean, he lives in *your* house?" she says.

"Do you want to come with us?" I ask.

"When are you going?"

"Next month."

A pause so short her answer was already in place. Like her resentment over so many things: my late marriage to Laura, the fawning attention we give Max, combined with my stiff-legged attempts to keep up with him, which only serve to reinforce her view that we are – or at least, at 58, I am – spectacularly unfit to parent at this age.

"I have finals," she says.

"So no?" I ask for confirmation.

"Yes, no."

I am relieved. I have come close to maxing out my Discover card. I expect a few other credit cards will get maxed out before our trip is over.

"I'm sorry," I say.

"Not surprising," she says. "You didn't ask me when would be convenient for me."

Other sources of resentment: she and Thurman are separated by an ocean; that I didn't force her to learn French as my mother had done to me. I forced her to grow up in a city, ignoring her love of the outdoors.

"It's the only time that works for the rest of us," I say. "After, I have to prep for my company's user conference, it works for Thurman, and Laura can visit a customer in Estonia."

In other words, I have no real reason for not having invited her other than I didn't think of it until it was too late.

"Okay," Clara says. "One more family non-event I'm not a part of."

"At least I didn't put you in a foster home," I try to joke, at my mother's expense.

"Not funny," Clara says.

5

THE LEMON AND THE LIME

Thurman is supposed to meet us at Charles de Gaulle airport, but he's late.

"Where's Turman?" Max asks, dropping the "h." If he weren't only three years old, I'd think he was mocking my choice of a name: the French can't pronounce the "th" sound either.

"He'll be here," I say, slightly irritated at Thurman for being late.

"Where is he?" Max stretches his legs out of his stroller and kicks.

"He's on the way."

"But where is he?"

"Good question," Laura says.

My temper is soothed by the familiarity of the ambient sounds. Public announcements are in French, people make funny sounds in the backs of their throats, and baristas at the airport bistro violently pound used grinds from the filter basket into a wooden drawer under the hissing espresso machine.

"He's on the Metro," I say.

"The metro? What's the metro?"

"It's a kind of train. Light rail."

Max spies him before we do. His expression suddenly goes from confused to lit up with pure joy, mouth open and blue eyes bright. His long lost older brother, someone mysterious who smells familiar and makes funny noises. A live, giant bearded bear to play with.

I want to get this right. What I screwed up between Clara and Thurman, I want to get right with Max.

Thurman hugs me and then Laura, and then goes to a knee to hug Max in his stroller. Max throws his arms around Thurman's neck and buries his nose in his older brother's hair, inhaling deeply.

I ride up front with the driver, Laura and Thurman in the back with Max between them. My mother's ashes are at Laura's feet, in the can of Swee-Touch-Nee tea she loved so much. I hope to find them a final resting place here in France, where she spent so much of her youth.

In my briefcase also between my feet, I have a bunch of work-related folders, my laptop, and a couple of folders from my mother's metal box. I figure I will have more time to look them over while I'm over here, and perhaps unearth a few more treasures.

It turns out that Thurman is heartbroken. His girlfriend Victoria ditched him before moving to Slovakia. He feels like she used him to get through the last few months until she moved, and that she led him to believe she felt more for him than she did.

"We were at a party one of the last evenings, and she said to some friends, right in front of me, 'there's nothing holding me back in France.' One of my friends took me aside and asked, 'why would she say something like that in front of you?' I was trying to find an excuse for her, but I'm tired of just being, I don't know, ignored," he says. "So you know, forget about her."

I turn my head to look at the expression in his face. He's smiling. He's trying to dismiss the matter, but it's just as heartbreaking for him in the retelling as it was in the moment.

"That's too bad," I say. "I liked Victoria."

"You never met her."

"Yes, but she had the same name as your grandmother – it made it easier for me to remember."

He chuckles, but I can tell it doesn't lighten his mood. I think he knows me well enough to know my jokes are just a way of making him feel better. Empathy through dark humor.

Laura scowls at me – it seems like another aspect of my personality she has grown to dislike.

Thurman was my best man at my wedding to Laura, which we held at a small boutique hotel in Rhinebeck, NY.

Two of Laura's friends got off the train from New York already drunk, and caused a ruckus in the hotel room just under our honeymoon suite. Laura was nervously trying to fit into her grandmother's wedding dress. She was gorgeous, but the racket made by her friends in the suite downstairs did nothing to calm her nerves.

I started pacing angrily in my nifty blue Ralph Lauren suit, a beautifully paired yellow tie flapping in the wind of my agitation. "Jesus, can they pipe down?" I said.

Then, seeing I was only making things worse for Laura, I decided to go downstairs. I stopped on my way down and confronted them.

"You couldn't at least wait until you got here before getting drunk, so you wouldn't act like a bunch of wedding crashers?" I shouted.

Then I went to the lobby where I found Thurman and had a drink with him. I looked at myself in the floor-to-ceiling mirror at the far end of the bar that separated the bar from the ballroom, and I didn't especially like what I saw.

"I've put on weight," I said.

"Don't worry, dad," Thurman said as he patted me on the shoulder. "You're a very handsome man."

Maybe it's the location – the foothills of the Catskill mountains, where I spent so many summers of my youth. Or maybe it's my age – I'm as old as my father was when I was born. Maybe it's that even on this, my wedding day, something feels incomplete, as if there were something I haven't accounted for, but that is looming.

I suddenly remember a time my father slapped me. He was dying, almost dead, on his last hurrah. A family vacation at a time when no kid wants any part of a family vacation, when friends are more interesting and girls are infinitely more interesting and there could be baseball to be watched instead of being with a couple of old people, one of them dying of cancer of the bladder, at a semi-secluded vacation rental called Orchard Colony, a half-dozen whitewashed bungalows off a two-lane in the Catskills, mostly empty and a few of them rented out to either octogenarian ladies, or a reclusive gay couple who dare not speak their love. No other kids to play with.

Ours was the bungalow closest to the road, across from which was a concrete handball court, the asphalt pavement fractured and tufted with weeds. I spent hours there, bouncing a Spaldeen against the wall, making incredible over-the-shoulder catches to the roar of the crowd noises I produced on my own.

Early one morning of that drab week, my mother called to me from the kitchen, rousing me from unremembered dreams to say the table wasn't set for breakfast.

My father was shaving, because a human being shaves every day. He suspenders hung in loops alongside his legs, and he was still in a pajama shirt.

"It won't be set if you don't set it," my mother repeated.

"I don't care," I said groggily.

I swung my legs off my bed and walked into the small kitchen, intending to comply. My father, shaving cream covering half his face, scowling furiously, crossed the room and confronted me, his suspenders swinging wildly.

"You don't care? You don't care about your mother?"

I opened my mouth, but it was too late.

He swung his arm and slapped my face. His arm kept going – I noticed he had a nice follow-through. My face hurt like hell, but I knew better than to cry in front of him. His arm came around again. Whap! This time he hit me with the back of his hand, and he seemed to hop a little on impact, as if he were putting his legs into it. And he wasn't done. His arm came around and he hit me again, shaving cream flying off his face. Just stand there and take it, I thought. Fractals of light appeared before me as unwanted tears welled below my eyelids.

The slaps came without undo haste, and even though his eyes

were pointed in my direction, not once did it seem as if he were actually looking at me. He seemed to be looking back in time, at what I couldn't guess. Not then.

At the time, I thought this had all been brought on by a misunderstanding. It never occurred to me that his rage wasn't commensurate with the moment. I knew it wasn't just about that moment. My mistake was in thinking it was remotely about me.

"Both of you! You deserve each other," Vivi shouted. "You are complete idiots." She stormed out of the kitchen – and straight out of the bungalow.

"Look how you make your mother speak to me," he said after a moment.

I realized how dangerous it would have been to laugh.

My mother reappeared after a few moments, brandishing a large stick she'd found in the grass.

"To chase away the wild dogs," she said.

"Where are you going, Vivi?" he asked.

"Away, I am going away."

And away she went. To exile. Again. Russia, France, Mexico, New York, and now... the wilderness! The terrible, untamed, 1970s American wilderness.

My father spent the rest of the morning in a white Adirondack chair, his back pressed against the wooden slats, his legs crossed above the knee in the European manner, his suspenders looped elegantly over his bony shoulders. He peered through thick glasses at the Week in Review section of the most recent Sunday *New York Times*, often closing his eyes with fatigue.

I banged the Spaldeen off the wall.

He never so much as scowled at me. Maybe, I thought, I'm already dead to him.

Now, 40 years later and 10 miles down the road, here I am getting married. Again. And trying not to slap anyone, without a clue as to why this sudden, disproportionate fury rises up inside of me, seemingly out of nowhere.

Later, Thurman gave his best man's speech, in an English inflected with French syntax that throws meaning into a different kind of relief:

"I think we all learn a way of loving others, and my father has his own way. He does not fear about opinions, distances and obstacles, because he's got a reckless way of loving.

"I've met Laura only a few months ago, but I already know she is a great lady, made of golden kindness and generosity. I see the way my father is looking at her and the way she is looking at him. This is a family. And not every kind of family. People who pay the price of the last century with their body and their soul. And in spite of it, we have two persons looking at each other with love, strength and tenderness. Is it a miracle? Is it just improbable? I absolutely do not know. But today, we are friends, and we share it. Thanks to Laura, thanks to my father, thanks to their way of loving each other."

I was glad I didn't have to respond, because I know my voice would have fractured and broken into sobs.

Later, Darren Lightfoot, my best friend from college, gave one of those speeches you cringe about in movies, with references to past wives and numerous other excesses. I wanted to remind him that Liz, ex-wife number two, was also in the room, making sure my mother was comfortable in her wheelchair and 80-something years.

Darren said, "Laura, whenever Michael raises his voice a tad too much, just remember, he doesn't realize how big he is or how loud he is. Big heart, big mouth, big everything – or so I hear."

Hah-hah.

Later that evening, Laura and I were swaying together on the dance floor, our friends no longer paying us mind, as their attentions fragmented into little clumps of shared interest and mutual discovery. A couple of single women hovered around Thurman, who ended up spending the night with one of Laura's drunk friends.

"Thurman's speech," I said as Laura rested her head on my shoulder.

"Oh my god, I was barely able to keep it together," she said, lifting her head. "Darren, on the other hand. Although he nailed you on your temper," she smiled.

"He also said I don't realize how loud I can be," I said.

She leaned into me, happy in the moment, happy enough to let the matter drift.

"Can you help me with something?" Thurman says as the taxi makes its way slowly down the A1 highway into Paris, past the graffiti splattered or stenciled onto every overpass, reflecting dueling expressions of Arab anger and white nationalist resentment.

"I need a ride to mom's house to get my belongings."

I steal a look at Laura, who is staring out the window. It means saddling her with Max for a day, but there's no way I'm going to refuse this request. It's a chance to put the final nail in the relationship between Thurman and his mother Brigitte.

I think back to the first week of my romance with Brigitte, days that blur together into a single afternoon of lovemaking, of realizing we love and hate the same artists, of sitting in cafés, watching other couples and inventing their lives for them.

Brigitte had me listen to Serge Gainsbourg about Harley Davidson motorcycles, sung by her namesake Brigitte Bardot. It's a song about the freedom of riding a Harley with the wind in your hair, not caring if you crash and spill your brains out on the Champs-Élysées because you've had this moment of catharsis like a huge metal cock between your legs.

"It's a stupid song sung by a stupid woman," Brigitte said. "Now that she's old, you can see the stupidity in the lines of her face."

She hated her mother for saddling her with the name of France's most enduring sex symbol.

She was a graphic designer who double-majored in fine arts and computer science. She got a contract from the French national robotics institute to beta-test their various computer-aided design and animation programs.

Later, she landed a contract with CanalPlus, the first private cable channel in France, for 10 episodes of an animated soap opera. They cut her loose when she missed the deadline for the second episode, but that's not why they cancelled her contract. Lots of people miss their deadlines. They killed it because her relationships soured. Because no one could live up to her expectations of them, and they grew tired of trying.

"You make me so sad," I overheard her telling her producer over the phone. "I thought you were special, but you're just like all the other people."

She uttered the word "people" as if she had said "dog turds."

Someone I knew in Paris during our honeymoon phase looked at a picture of her and told me to enjoy it while it lasted, because a guy like me could never hold onto a woman like that. I hated him for saying it, but it turned out he was right – not because of the many things that were wrong with me, but because I was never able to live up to her belief in my unique specialness.

We were lucky she got pregnant with Thurman during that very brief moment when our flames were burning at the same height, with the same heat, flickering in the same nurturing breeze.

"You know why no computer will ever pass the Turing test?" she said when we were still on good terms. The Turing test, I learned later, is simply the idea that you wouldn't be able to tell if you're talking to a computer instead of another human.

"Why not?" I asked.

"Because an artificial intelligence can never understand why a color is sad or joyful. Why is yellow happy? A computer could never say, but I can say yellow is happy because that was the color of the day when we met."

Now, she's become a shut-in, and lives in a fortress-like concrete former water mill in a small town 1,000 miles from everywhere, where she decided to raise Thurman after I left France.

The locals refer to the area as the Green Desert – it's a lush countryside with the population density of Montana. The landscape is flat and aqueous. The closest high school is an hour away – Thurman boarded there during the week and went home on weekends, where he told me he was even lonelier than when he was in his dorm room at school.

He excelled in high school, and got into the most prestigious university in France, *Sciences Po*.

After graduating, he launched a startup to save bees that fostered cooperation between bee keepers, farmers and small town governments to eliminate pesticides, help beekeepers monetize honey-based products, and organized educational trips to local apiaries.

Later, he launched a social media platform to help people find like-minded social do-gooders. Unfortunately, it wasn't a good platform for sex hook-ups, so it foundered. Now he's looking for his next opportunity to remake the world.

I'm proud of him, confident in his ability.

Thurman and his mother haven't spoken in more than a year. I should be concerned, but I'm secretly triumphant.

We're staying with my friend the actor Philippe Fresnay, who is lending us his apartment while he's on location in the south of France. His apartment is close to the Bastille neighborhood, the symbolic center of the French Revolution – and of democracy itself. The streets are narrow, still cobblestoned in some cases, twisting curlicues promising a new café or surprising little shop around every bend.

I've known Philippe since we were both in the beginning phases of whatever it is that we're doing. He finally broke through as a movie actor thanks to a role that had no lines at all. But his looming, hulking presence didn't go unnoticed by casting directors. He has since won acting awards, been featured in long-running TV series, and gets his share of roles on US film productions because he can speak enough English to play a French bad guy or a cop (or sometimes both).

He's rough-looking, with a pock-marked round face, sandy hair carefully combed to hide some thinning, and is taller than most Frenchmen. He is, of course, an incredibly sweet guy. It being France, he dated Brigitte for a couple of years after she and I broke up, before she dumped him and took up with a Keith Haring knock-off artist.

"You never gave me any grief, you never said anything bad about Brigitte, while I was with her," Philippe said after their split.

"To tell you the truth, I was relieved, for Thurman's sake. I knew you'd be good with him," I said.

We had been friends before, we've become closer as time went on, and we don't discuss her very often.

Philippe is at the apartment when we arrive; he hands me the keys and shows us around.

"I'm driving Thurman to Brévaq," I say. "To pick up his stuff."

Philippe looks concerned. "Are you going to tell her you're coming?" he asks.

"Yes," Thurman says.

"Good, because she might not take it very well if you just showed up unannounced."

After dropping our bags, Laura, Thurman and I walk out of the apartment, pushing Max in his stroller into the heart of the popular Bastille neighborhood. Most of the buildings are hundreds of years old, with ancient wooden porticos hiding cobblestone courtyards that sprawl out into honeycombs of other courtyards and buildings, most of which were occupied by tradespeople engaged in cabinet-making, lamp manufacturing, and other light industries. Today, many of those businesses have been replaced by architectural firms, creative agencies, and other liberal arts professions.

There's a sheen of modernity, of shingles with sans-serif fonts, layered over centuries of sawdust, sweat, and craftsmanship; of eras overlapping as sleek office workers slip past burly mattress makers still plying their ancient trade, the smart set in tight clothes sharing a bar counter with workers in "bleue de travail" blue coveralls.

There are tons of cafés, bistros, restaurants, and bars, all of them teeming with customers at all times of the day, and of course at night. I lived in this neighborhood when I was dating Brigitte, and the smells of beer, sweat, stale tobacco and peed-on walls are as Elmer's Glue to primary school; the inchoate memories of anticipation, freedom, ashtrays, women, music, and alienation flood through me. I thought I would live here forever.

It's lunchtime, and we stop at a small bistro on rue de la Roquette, the narrow main artery of the Bastille.

Our waitress is a slender blond woman named Ebba, and from her accent it's obvious she's not French.

"Irish?" I ask.

"Swedish," comes the reply.

Throughout the course of the meal, she takes an obvious shine to Thurman, and I egg him on like any obnoxious parent. He's not shy, but he's modest.

Over lunch, I lay out our itinerary for Thurman. I try to tamp down my excitement, but I feel my voice rising in pitch and volume as I talk about the factory, seeing where my father grew up, finding out more about him – and sizing up the situation from a legal perspective.

"I've already asked about restitution. There are a lot of potential avenues for that. But I also want to see it for myself," I say.

"But you're not a lawyer," Thurman says. "Especially not a German lawyer." He smiles.

"No, but I want to determine some basic facts. You know, how thick is the wall in case we have to storm the castle. Is there an underground tunnel? That kind of thing."

I take Max to the bathroom, and when I get back, Thurman has taken a picture of a slice of lemon borrowed from my iced tea, a lime from Laura's dessert, and a drinking straw. He and Laura are laughing at it.

"What's so funny?" Ebba asks as she clears some plates.

He holds his phone up for her to see the screen. "It's the lemon and the lime," he says. "They're having an adventure."

She laughs, her voice tinkling with pleasure and intelligence. "Oh good, I thought you were making fun of the way I walk."

People are often self-conscious about things no one else even notices.

"No, it's a piece of art. It's for you – would you like me to send it to you?"

"I'd love it," she says. She glides to the kitchen to pick up another order.

"You have her phone number?" I ask Thurman.

He shakes his head.

"Then how are you supposed to send it to her?"

"Good point," he says.

I wait for him to pop the question when she drops off our check, but he doesn't say anything. I pull my wallet out and put down a few euros.

"Do you need change?" she asks when she swoops back to our table.

"No, but how is Thurman supposed to give you the picture if he doesn't have, I don't know, a phone number or an email address?"

She laughs.

"Dad," he complains.

He can't understand. I no longer hit on women, I no longer have the pleasure of measuring myself against my own fear of speaking to women I don't know, of being rejected. I no longer have the rush of joy that comes with even the slightest success – the smile, the phone number given, the date accepted. I live vicariously through his flirting, as probably millions of fathers have done through the ages.

Ebba leans over and whispers to him, and he types as she talks.

Laura and I push Max in his stroller outside to give them some space.

Thurman meets us on the narrow sidewalk. "She said she's never had a father pimp out his son to her before."

"Oh shit," I say, and I feel my cheeks flush.

"No, she thinks it's funny."

"Did you make a date?"

"Dad. I'll take it from here," he says. "I have my own way of doing this, you know."

Yeah, I think. Your way would have been to walk out of there without so much as her phone number.

I sit in Pierre's apartment while Max is napping, thinking about Germany and what I will find there, and what sort of reception I'll receive. I Google the names of lawyers specialized in European affairs, the recovery of works of art looted by the Nazis, or reparations. I check the Kupfer factory website obsessively: 135 years.

Laura flies to visit her client in Estonia for a couple of days, leaving Thurman and me to take care of Max. It's the first real solid I've done her in ages, and it's a relief. I'm not good at doing this sort of thing spontaneously – I have to be asked. But once asked, I'm more than happy to oblige. It helps me avoid being a complete and utter asshole.

My boss Jessica calls early on the first afternoon of Laura's absence – early morning east coast time. "Hickins, you've been very MIA lately," she says. "And our friends in marketing say you're finding lots of excuses for not writing their customer stories."

She doesn't realize I'm being consumed by a question that is suddenly overwhelming my consciousness, and she wouldn't care if she did. "So, are you?" she says.

"Am I what?"

"Collaborating."

I think about that word – how it's lost its historical significance – the opprobrium of that word, which was synonymous with Nazi sympathizing, with aiding and abetting the subjugation of countries invaded by the Axis power, of sleeping with the enemy, of ratting out

Jews and Communists and settling scores with rivals and selling food on the black market.

Collabo.

A few hours later, my sister Bette calls, unaware I'm overseas.

I'd sent her a share of the money from the sale of mother's cabin, but she still needs more, and I send her a small stipend every week. I've taken care of her for as long as I've been able. It sometimes pisses me off, but I love her. She might be the only person I've ever loved with no expectation of anything in return except feeling good about myself.

Maybe that's the only return worth hoping for.

"The house is flooding because of all the rain," she says. "They're calling it a hundred-year rain, but it seems like it's happening every year now. Anyway, I had to get them to deliver gravel for the driveway, and it cost almost five thousand dollars."

"How much do you need?" I ask.

"I get paid next Thursday. I need $17 for gas and like another $10 for the animal pantry, and I owe six dollars for garbage pickup, so I guess $33."

I try to keep the annoyance out of my voice when I say "okay." I'm less annoyed by the amount than the enumeration of needs.

Or that when she says "get paid," she makes it sound like she's got a job. She doesn't. It's her social security check, pathetic though it is – barely enough to cover the mortgage on her house, for which she paid too much and which she will never be able to sell.

I can't get through the irony that she doesn't make enough to cover her mortgage for a one bedroom in the middle of nowhere, not to mention her diabetes medication, and her other basic needs, but is nevertheless considered too well off to qualify for Medicaid. Meanwhile, here in France, her meds would be covered and she'd be getting at least a universal basic income. So we punish the working poor by forcing them into begging from family once they're too old, too sick or too weak to continue working. That's one hell of a work ethic.

"I can pay you back," she says.

"Don't be ridiculous," I snap, failing to sound remotely even-tempered. "You're just going to have to borrow more from me – just skip it."

This is one reason I gave up on journalism and took this ridiculous job writing speeches and op-eds for a giant software company.

Bette says, "I love you, kiddo, and not just because you're giving me money."

"I love you too," I say.

I was three years old and crying in my room because I wanted to eat more cherries than my father said I could have before bed – something about it being bad for my stomach at such a young age. Bette would have been 20. She came in and sat on the edge of my bed. She promised to buy me a toy if I calmed down.

Later, I heard her in the dining room, telling my mother and father what she had done to quiet me down.

"I will not have you bribing the child," my father said.

"I gave him my word," she said.

I fell asleep to the sound of their quarrel.

The next morning, she walked me to Genovese Drugs on 82nd street in Jackson Heights, close to the Jackson movie theater and the fire station, where she bought me a toy.

She defied the lawgiver that was my father to defend my interests. That would be to her credit for the rest of our lives.

———————

Thurman and I take Max to the playground and let him climb on park equipment meant for kids twice his age. We find a bench in the shade, next to a pair of Muslim women dressed head-to-toe in black.

"I guess we're in a no-go zone," I joke.

"Yes, the terrorists are winning," Thurman responds.

Then he opens his little denim man-purse and takes out a lemon and a lime. He grins at me, places them on the bench next to us, snaps a picture.

On the way back to Philippe's apartment, I check out the car rental storefronts as we walk along the boulevard Voltaire, trying to estimate the size of the van we'll need for the trip to his mother's home in Brévaq.

In addition to picking up his own stuff, which he figures will fit into six or seven boxes, Thurman has promised to swing by the cabinet-making factory owned by the family of his longtime buddy Florent to pick up a couple of boxes from there too.

"Why don't you use Blahblahcar?" Thurman asks.

"Is that a real thing?"

"Yes," he laughs.

A short time later, Thurman stops me on the sidewalk and puts the lemon down on the ground. Then he scavenges a garbage can for a piece of cardboard, and places it next to the lemon. He puts a few coins on the cardboard and snaps a picture with his smartphone. Next he pulls out the lime and places it a few steps away from the lemon, and snaps another picture. He moves the lime closer to the lemon and takes another snapshot.

"The lemon has no more hope," he explains. "He's begging money to go on a road trip, but he doesn't know where he's going or if he's ever coming back.

"The lime says he will accompany him. The lemon says, 'no, I have no hope, no friends, just leave me alone.' But the lime says they can be friends, they can go on the road together. 'I have no friends either, let us see what the future holds for both of us', the lime says."

Thurman places the lemon and the lime next to one another on the sidewalk and takes a couple of pictures, one close up and the other a long shot.

Later that evening, sitting on a modern, uncomfortable couch in Philippe's apartment, I download the Blahblahcar app and find a cheap utility vehicle that will do the job quite nicely.

"You're sure this app is legit?" I ask Thurman.

"Sure," he says.

But what does he know? He still uses a Blackberry, doesn't drive or have a license, and notwithstanding the failed Internet business he started with so much promise, he seems in so many ways stuck in the pre-Internet days. It's not so much about gizmos or apps he has or doesn't have as his attitude, which is cautious and reserved. He is not trusting of what the hucksters of the day are selling.

I'm looking forward to the long drive together, just the two of us. The symbolism of helping him leave his mother isn't lost on me either. Me of the trail of family members littered all over the fucking place, as Clara puts it.

6

YOU'RE A RIGHT BASTARD

The app won't even tell me where the car is parked until the morning of the day we're leaving. We've planned to get on the road at six, before Paris traffic snarls us in its sticky web. I kiss Laura softly so as to not awaken Max. Thurman and I snick the apartment door shut and walk towards the general vicinity of the car; more precise geolocation eventually guides us to the street where it's parked, and we finally identify the small truck. Now I worry I didn't pick a large enough vehicle.

It has all the creature comforts of a Flintstone car. I would shout "yabba dabba do!" but Thurman wouldn't get the joke.

We've already agreed that he's going in there alone – in fact, I'm going to drop him off where we hope his mother can't see me, and he'll send me a text message when he's ready to load the van with his boxes. She's expecting Thurman, but she's not expecting to see me, and it might not be a good thing if she did.

It's a two-and-a-half hour drive, and after an hour, we stop for coffee at a glam truck stop. I say glam because it's France, and the vending machines offer bouillabaisse, roast duck, and chocolate mousse. Sure, you can just get a sandwich – but it's with Brie and fresh roasted organic chicken.

Thurman excuses himself and goes to the bathroom, where he

takes a picture of the lemon and the lime sharing a cigarette. He sits back down across the table from me and shows me the picture on his phone.

"It's easier to see where the road leads when you're together than when you're alone," Thurman says.

He's talking about the lemon and the lime, but he could be talking about himself.

I think about the lonely road he's been on his whole life. "I'm sorry about all that," I say.

He smiles at me. "About all what?"

"Making your own breakfast, taking yourself to school."

He laughs like I don't know the half of it. He's probably right. Even knowing Brigitte was crazy, I believed she loved him more than anything; that for all her anti-social instincts, she would provide him with warmth and mothering. I'd like to think I wouldn't have left him in her care and moved back to the US if I had known the truth. But I cannot know that any more than I can undo the past.

"There were days I missed the school bus, and since mom doesn't have a driver's license, I'd go to the café and ask if someone could drive me to school. There was always someone. He'd put down his glass of wine on the counter, and Rene the barman would say, 'I'll buy you another glass when you get back,' and the guy would drive me to school."

Thinking we're lucky none of those drunks were perverts.

He gets a text message from Ebba the Swedish waitress. He has managed to compile "The Lemon But the Lime" into a sort of photo-montage, complete with subtitles.

He holds his phone up so I can read her response as I'm driving: *This is literally the best thing I've ever seen.* I can hear her Swedish-accented English in my head.

Thurman exchanges texts with her for a few more kilometers. She gets off work at 1 am, and he wants to know if we'll be back in Paris by then.

"I sure as fuck hope so," I say.

Not only do I want to be back to help Laura put Max to bed, which is unlikely but possible – but I want Thurman to score with Ebba. It will put Victoria in the rear view mirror for good, and will put him in a much better mood for our long drive to Ansbach.

"Why is it 'the Lemon *but* the Lime' instead of 'The Lemon *and* the Lime?'" I ask.

"Because the lemon was headed for doom, until the lime arrived. So the lemon was sad, but the lime made him happy."

"They're both male?"

"It doesn't matter, so long as they are happy," he says.

I see signs for Dijon – the capital of Burgundy, and probably the northern-most city of what was once called Free France – the unoccupied south of what remained of France after it capitulated and the Germans rolled in with their tanks and their anti-Semitic laws.

"Was there a lot of resistance activity in Dijon?" I ask Thurman.

"How should I know?"

"Well, you went to Sciences Po. You studied French history and politics."

"You studied literature at Columbia. Do you know everything about English literature?"

I'm a little surprised at his tone. I am under the impression things are good between us. Maybe he's more nervous about seeing his mother than he's letting on. I've written her off, and she was never my flesh and blood, so it's easy for me to let go of her. As long as I'm not in physical danger from her, everything is fine – I have nothing to worry about.

I only have one emotion – the anticipation of a final victory. His bitter sadness is the furthest thing from my mind. I am snapped back to the reality of his life: His mother doesn't care a damn about him.

"Burgundy was too rich, always too rich to worry about things like fighting for justice," he says finally. "The dukes of Burgundy were even richer than the kings of France. During the war, everywhere in

France there was penury. The Germans devalued the franc by 20 percent against the Reichsmark, which made everything, even bread, impossibly expensive. But Burgundy never suffered. It had no need for resistance."

My mother's ashes are still in the can of Swee-Touch-Nee Tea, sitting next to the gear shift on the floor between us. I'm thinking that maybe we find a good spot to scatter them, someplace relevant, someplace that would have meant something to her.

I think about my mother's journey here in France. Her parents moved to Paris in the spring of 1923, when she was three months old. She grew up speaking Russian at home and French everywhere else. Her father was a labor lawyer who wasn't Communist enough for Lenin, and whose stilted French wasn't good enough to allow him entry to the Paris bar. He worked facilitating foreign transactions for Credit Lyonnais, a big French bank, until the Nazis overran France.

Her brother Georges, whom she venerated, was killed near Verdun on the day before the French surrendered. She mourned him all the rest of her life; his photograph always had pride of place on her bookshelves no matter where she lived.

Her parents sent her away from Paris, to the south, near the Spanish border, where she met a young Spanish refugee named Juan Antonio Castillo.

She got pregnant with Chris when she was 17; Johnny a year later. Both were born in France, near Toulouse. When they eventually moved to the US, to New York City, kids teased Chris and Johnny about the name of the place where they were born: To Lose.

Johnny broke a bottle on some kid's head over it when he was 10, which got him sent to juvie – before my mother put both boys in foster care.

———

I meet my niece Camille at the train station closest to our house. I've never met her before, but she's easy to spot: She's the one with the facial scarring and a streak of orange painted across her brow like a clementine-hued Lone Ranger mask. Her hair is a stiff, Mohawklength orangutan-orange. I settle my face into what I hope looks like a look of benign enthusiasm.

Not only have I never met her before, I never knew she existed until Luis found her too, just like he'd found me, though a mixture of Ancestry.com and persistence.

Unlike me, she's of his generation, sort of. She's his cousin – the only kid (so far as we know) of Chris, Johnnie's brother. No one knows where Chris has gone, or if he's even alive.

I get out of the car and open my arms. She is holding a large bouquet of wildflowers, a gift-wrapped package for Max, and a large, dangling handbag. We hug awkwardly, packages banging my sides and her small breasts flicking freely across my chest. She is wearing musky perfume. I peer down to verify; yup, no bra.

She sits in the passenger seat and we start the 20-minute drive to my house.

"I'm glad you were able to make it out here. People don't like coming out to the suburbs," I say.

"Oh, it was easy. It's not very far. I'm just glad it worked out. This famous tattoo artist from St. Petersburg was in NY and I was able to get an appointment. I was one of the lucky ones."

"Your grandmother was from St. Petersburg," I say.

"Oh wow! What a coincidence."

"The world is full of them."

"Did it hurt?"

"I'm used to them by now. I have more than 20 tats," she says.

I want to look, but also the road is a twisty two-lane, and there's still a layer of frost over the dingy snow.

"Plus I have all the time of the world now. I lost custody of my two babies, so I can travel. I'm remodeling this house I bought in Daytona. I figure if I don't have to keep the kids in-state, I might as well move somewhere where it's warm."

"Your ex-husband lives in Oregon?"

She nods. "Sam – my oldest – decided he wanted to live with his dad, which is cool. I respect that. He just doesn't have all the facts."

I nod. "You have a lot in common with your aunt Bette," I say.

"She has a lot of tats?"

I laugh. "No, none that I know of. No, she lost her kids in a custody fight too. They said she was too poor and, um, she'd been in a psych ward for a few months."

Camille doesn't say anything.

"My ex and I were in the lifestyle, you know? B&D, we had a dungeon in our house, the works. Then he shows Sam some pictures of me in the garb, and my son says, 'my mother's a whore, I don't want to live with a whore.'"

"I thought your husband was in it too."

"Yeah, but he's a man. The rules are different."

I sneak a look at her.

"It's true," she says. "That's what the asshole judge in Oregon said. 'The rules are different, young lady.'"

"Damn," I say. "In this day and age."

"Yeah, but I get to the see them a lot. It's fine. I get to travel. I just got back from a trip to Mexico where I did a detox retreat to fight Lyme's Disease. It's in remission but most people don't realize you need to detoxify or it just comes right back."

"There's a lot of Lyme's Disease around here."

"Global warming," she says. "It's everywhere. I got it in Utah."

"What were you doing in Utah?"

"God, long story. My mother was raped when she was 14, and no one believed her. So when I was 14 she sent me to Utah to live with the Mormons."

"Because?" I'm smiling.

"Because Mormons never rape anyone," she says, laughing.

"Was it okay?"

"It's where I met my husband," she says.

"The one who was in the life with you?"

"The lifestyle, yeah. Bunch of kinky motherfuckers," she says. "I really loved my family. They were awesome. And then they just cut me off. So I went home and found my mother had thrown out all my shit without even telling me. But I always knew she disapproved of me."

"What do you mean?"

"The tattoos, the lifestyle. I said, 'mom, people are going to stare at me no matter what I do. I might as well have them stare at me on their own terms."

We're pulling into the driveway of my house.

"I earn good money as a sex therapist and clown, and I have the settlement from the car company. I just want you to know I don't want anything from you, except a connection."

I put the car in park and look at her directly. "I wasn't worried," I say.

———

Max greets us at the door.

Act normal. This is a perfectly normal situation. Aunt Camille is a tattoo jigsaw puzzle and those are her nipples – happens all the time.

Camille's present for Max is a box of self-clumping dirt he can build stuff with. Just like kitty litter, only more adhesive and less smelly.

I hate to tell her, but he was probably hoping for some dinosaurs – his favorite "animal."

———

If I were a three-year-old, I might ask how come I've never met my Aunt Camille before, or why you've never met her, or whether we'll ever see her again. But we will see her again. I'm going to make sure of that. I'm going to change the family pattern just like Superman bending the course of mighty rivers. By sheer force of will.

Like Luis, Camille has never met her father. Never seen so much as a photograph. He was a six-month shooting star in her mother's life, a man on a motorcycle who stayed through the seventh month of her pregnancy and left her with a note that said simply, "I love you but I can't do this."

Stories from his past: his first wife, Angie, died during a late miscarriage in 1967. He served in the Navy in 1959. He lived in a foster home until he joined the service. He was circumcised when he was 13 years old.

I reel at the thought.

How did it come to this, that two people have lived into adulthood without so much as seeing a picture of their fathers? What links them, of course, is my mother, Vivi. Viviane Bronstein Castillo Hickins was both their grandmother. What the hell happened to her?

Carol and I caught her in a reflective mood one evening, a few weeks before she died. Maybe we knew she didn't have long, although Vivi and I had been expecting her imminent death for more than 20 years, even before she moved into her damn cabin in the woods.

She started talking about what she did in the south of France during the war in the '39 and '40, and her first husband, Juan Antonio, the son of Spanish Republicans.

"Get your phone and record this," Laura whispered.

Q: When you left France, how did you get away from the German sub?

I was not part of the action, I didn't shoot at the submarine. We were stopped and some military people came aboard and apparently there was nobody of interest. It was a Portuguese ship. Maybe they had an interest in finding some of the Spaniards on board because they were Republicans, but I don't know. They didn't take anybody. Apparently they inspected everything they were supposed to inspect. Maybe they were looking for armaments or they were looking for a particular spy. We were let go.

Q: Were you nervous?

No, it was all an adventure! I was 18 – what do you want? At that age, everything is an adventure.

. . .

Q: So you ended up in Mexico City?

My father through his political thing had arranged for emergency visas for the whole family, except for Juan Antonio because at the time he made the arrangements there was no Juan Antonio. Maybe he thought if he ignored him, he would not be there. I don't know, I can't ascribe motives to my father post-factum. But anyhow, Juan Antonio did not have a visa for the United States, so an emergency visa was arranged for the whole bunch of us to go to Mexico with the idea that from Mexico we could get to New York where my parents were, but Juan Antonio and I liked it in Mexico, and for him the language was there, and he had his diplomas in agronomical engineering or whatever, and that was supposed to be his profession.

I started working at the Institut Française de l'Amérique Latine, *teaching French literature, and I went to the University of Mexico studying anthropology and the history of the country, and at the same time I started doing work in the theater in Spanish and French also, because we had a French community there. So I was happy to be in Mexico, and I made many friends there and I grew very much apart from Juan Antonio, and so that was the Mexican thing. That's where Bette and Paulette were born.*

And things became very bad between me and Juan Antonio, so I decided to go visit my father who was in New York, and he was sick – he had a heart condition – and I told Juan Antonio I just wanted to visit my father, and he understood that. And he had to authorize me because in Mexico the husband had to authorize the wife to travel abroad and to take his children with her.

So I decided I was enough of an actress to make him think I was going to come back, so I left all my books and my records and the things that were really close to my heart and most of my clothes, you know, just took the kids and traveled.

Q: Did something happen to Johnnie in Mexico or was he just born crazy?

. . .

Johnnie was always crazy, it's the truth. He was. When he was about one or two years old, he crawled into Chris's bed to shit there. He really had to crawl in – he had a child's bed, but he really had to climb in and out of it. But he really hated that brother of his for being older, you know. Chris was such a pacific kid, a wonderful kid. It wouldn't have occurred to him to do any harm to the little brother. Johnnie was always a little bit strange. Very good looking.

Q: The minute he was born, could you tell?

No, he didn't look crazy. He was very possessive, he wanted his mother only to himself, and he resented the fact that he was not the only one there, and that there had been one already there before him, so he punished him. What else is one to do?

No, he was a nasty little boy, but people didn't see it right away because he was good looking and he could be very charming.

And then he bothered his sisters very much also. Teased them, was unpleasant to them. He would have been perfect as an only child.

Q: As I grow older, I find it harder to explain to people that I have two brothers that I never met.

They met you, I mean briefly. But I know what you're saying.

Q: What does that mean, they met you? Took one look and said, fuck it, we're out of here?

I had a brother. I'm quite sure he's no longer on this planet – this was Victor, my father's son from a previous marriage.

. . .

64

Q: But that's different. You were a little kid and your parents moved to another country and there was a war. Here, they just went to California and disappeared or something. There were probably years when I could have gone to visit Johnnie in prison.

You could – I don't think you would have wanted.

Q: It's bizarre that I didn't.

Well you know, he stayed very little in contact with me over the years. Once in a while when he needed something or wanted something or wanted to give the Navy an explanation for going AWOL, and of course they came to look for him and I said I don't know where he is.

Once in a while he wrote to me while he was in the Navy and he had bought some boots for Bette, Spanish leather embossed boots, and she was waiting to get them, and finally he wrote that he had sold them because he needed the money.

With Chris, it was a very strange thing because there were years and years when we corresponded a lot, and while he was in the Navy he was in the submarine and he liked being in the service and then he went to work related to the Navy in some oceanic research – I don't know in what capacity – but he was interested in marine science anyhow, so I don't know. And I had his address and then I didn't have it anymore then and then Jackie had it and then she didn't have it anymore.

And he lived in Hawaii and married a Japanese Hawaiian girl and they divorced after a few years and after that he didn't keep in touch anymore. There was no rupture per se, he just didn't continue and I didn't have his address. I made a few attempts to write to the Navy.

But dead or alive, I always felt a rapport with Chris, and I never felt there was a cutoff, you know. So whatever reason or lack of reason he had for not writing were his own, and I don't think he ever hated me. We had some misunderstandings but they were not deep enough to cause a rupture.

. . .

Q: Do you think Chris resented you for having been in a foster family?

Well, for a while, yes. But I think he got over that because he got to understand the circumstances which had forced the situation to exist. He knew that I had not chosen that situation. So this is why we became close again. As I told you too, I can't just love you because I'm your mother. At first, sure, every mother loves her cubs, wolves in the wild love their cubs. But then the cubs grow up, and if they're mean or not truthful or weak, that's it. Chris earned my love. Johnnie, poor guy. He didn't.

Q: It's hard because rationally okay, you can understand, you had to live with your parents four kids in a small apartment – that was the reason right?

That was one reason but it was not just the apartment, it was – I needed my parents' support – being there while I went to work. Somebody had to be there. My father way a sick man at that time, and he couldn't take the agitation of four kids coming and going, and all that. And so it was just my mother, and she did her very darndest also you know, but it was just too much. It was not just the size of the apartment.

Q: It's easy to understand rationally, but emotionally maybe...?

I know. Also, he knew that Johnnie was very much to blame for the situation at home, and that I could not just get rid of Johnnie.

But you know, when I said before I never regret anything I lived, it's true because me personally, I enjoyed my life. I know that not every member of my family felt the same way, but each person lives his own life in his own skin and I don't know why, but I always managed to find joy and happiness and love and all that, all the time.

Maybe I'm a very superficial person but I enjoy the moment.

Q: I wouldn't say that.

I glide over things, you know, I don't dwell in the negative. Sure, as I talk now, I have to face those negatives in order to explain things to you as much as I can but normally, by myself, I really don't dwell on these things. I don't, I couldn't live if I did. I don't know if I'm supposed to feel bad being a happy person.

I'm supposed to feel guilty for being happy?

I tuned off the recording because she seemed to be trailing off. She paused a long time, and then she started up again, so I picked it up again.

They were all such idealist and serious people, my mother and father, and all the Russians. Very proper and dignified. How did they get that girl? Meaning me. It came from my father. He was a little bit of the wild side, even though he had those high principles, he had the joie de vivre *also. On my mother's side, they were all much too serious to enjoy life.*

My father came to Roscoff on vacation and took off his clothes and just in his swim trunks walked on his hands on the beach. He said 'I had one season with the circus in Odessa.' I didn't know that. When he was a young adolescent, he ran away with the circus.

And in Paris he did not – and he could not – become a lawyer in France, he could not translate his credentials – he didn't want to, he was going to go back to Russia anytime. He was a great Russia patriot, but he had a bevy of young ladies, young Russian ladies, coming to the house to ask his advice. They knew he knew what they needed to know.

When I became almost a teenage girl I became very jealous and I didn't understand how my mother tolerated all these young beautiful women coming to the house, and she was telling me, 'you are such a child. You don't understand the relationship between people. Just because a man and a woman are together alone in a room doesn't mean anything of a sexual matter' – and you know she was very anatomical about it – 'people can relate intellectually no matter what gender they are.'

She was lecturing me and lecturing me and it was uncomfortable. She was so serious about everything, she lectured me, she was telling me when I became interested in the subject, 'sexual relationships are the most wonderful way to communicate between people.' It was liberal but it was intellectual-liberal.

Q: Did he get paid for any of this advice?

Of course not! My father did not mix business with pleasure! No, he was very honest.

My grandmother continued giving medical advice, she had all these old gossips coming for tea and sweets, she had her coterie and they all came with their ills because she had been their doctor over there so they continued ... of course she wouldn't charge them, she wasn't a practicing doctor in Paris. Those Russians were so high minded, I was never like that, I wanted to get paid for what I did.

Q: He worked in an automobile factory and then he had a hernia. Then what did he do?

He became chief accountant in the Credit Lyonnais. That was up to the war, he had a very good position there, he had always liked working with figures. He always had a feeling for business. His specialty was international law, so he was actually dealing with international business things, so I guess it makes sense that accounting was something he had an understanding for. Not me. He always told me when I was a kid that I should grow up to be my like my mother. He had a lot of respect for her. I knew I would never be able to, nor want to.

Like my grandmother, yes. But my grandmother discouraged me very early from wanting to be a doctor. She said I didn't have the temperament for it, that I would succumb to it emotionally.

For me it was a choice when I was very young – am I going to be a doctor or a lawyer? And the blah blah was more in my line.

I would have liked to know my brother Victor. I have pictures of him sitting on an ice floe. He did it for fun. That was sad for my father, not to be able to communicate with my brother – but that you can blame on outside stuff – revolutions and wars and political things. That's a clean cut thing.

On the other hand, I could never understand my mother. My mother's attitude toward my father's first marriage. He was still married when they met and he had that boy who was I think eight, and the only explanation she gave me – she said your father had grown away from his first wife, had matured over the years, and his wife hadn't. That's a pretty cold attitude. She was more rational than I am. I always reproached her in my innermost soul that she had been a home-breaker. He fell in love with her, and she with him, and he was married, and happily so until they met. But she rationalized it – he outgrew her like an old shoe. I guess those things do happen but you don't have to accept it and profit from it.

Victor wanted to stay with his mother when he learned his father was going to have to go into exile. He would have taken her also, it's not like he would have thrown her away, you know, but she didn't want to leave, she wanted to stay in Russia. She was not political and the boy wanted to stay with his mother.

Q: Not like your father.

No, I guess not like him. He was very political. He was also a labor lawyer, he used to tell me, "if you have a question about a policy or such and such, you ask yourself two questions. How does it affect the worker, and how does it affect the Jews?'

Q: That was the litmus test.

He was with the Mensheviks, you know, he was very committed. So when they told him he could stay in Russia, but 20 years in Siberia, or lifetime exile, he wanted to go to Siberia. But my mother was very pragmatic, she said 'oh, no.' So they took me to Paris to live.

My mother was very interested in Buddhism. She had all those books, which I read of course, about the life of Buddha and Buddhism in general, she was also a Freemason.

I discovered it quite by accident because it's supposed to be a secret society. I was rummaging through my father's desk – he had a big, heavy desk. Apparently one of the deep drawers was my mother's. And there I was going through and found the apron that they wear during ceremonies. I had never seen that – and of course I could not keep my mouth shut, I had to ask what is this. Oh the shock! 'What? Where did you find this?'

Then she told me what it was. 'You're not supposed to see it, it's a private thing, blah blah blah going through drawers.'

I found very interesting things in that desk. Another time I found a cigar that I smoked and I didn't know it wasn't an ordinary cigar – it had opium in it. It was an evening when they had gone out. I don't know why my father had it. My grandmother was in her room and I don't know where Georges was – he was still living at home. I smoked that in my room and ... ugh.. I didn't particularly like it but I had to try it.

George was the one who enlightened me afterwards, what it was.

How you can live at home with father, mother, and grandmother and still have adventures.

Camille blinks her lash-less eyelids, smiles her melted-lip smile at Max, trying to exude peace, tranquility, and love. She wants to be someone who is at peace with herself, with everyone, with the world, and not at all embittered by the cracker who still lives with her mother, the firecracker that lit her body on fire for years, the scars that she will carry on her carcass like a bad tattoo.

Camille's body is like a stigmata passed on from my mother to the next generation, or a giant middle finger that says, "you have no idea what I've suffered."

"I love my work. I love working with people and helping them come to terms with whatever turns them on. My particular kink is, I get off on tears," Camille says. "Watching men cry."

I nod because there is no other reaction possible. I myself am trying to exude peace, tranquility and love. And calmness. Laura is in the back room; I can only imagine what she's thinking.

"I have this fantasy," Camille says. "I'm fighting Chuck – the guy who lit the firecracker that turned me into this – and it's really bloody and the outcome is uncertain. And then this other me steps out of a limo and all you see at first is my leg, like a glamorous, high-heeled, sexy insect, and I get all the way out of the car and I have this glistening white exoskeleton that shoots white goo on his face and burns him alive in an acid bath. It gets me hot," she says.

But who turned her into this, really? Was it the cracker, or was it Belinda, her mom? Or Chris, who flaked out because he couldn't stand waiting to see if Belinda would die in childbirth like his first baby mama?

Or was it our mother Vivi who taught him that it's okay to flake on your children – put them in foster care, have them circumcised at the age of 13 in some paroxysm of religious guilt, argue that parental love is conditional – or was it the war and its unspoken bloody aftermath?

Thurman and I get off the highway and take smaller roads to the village of Crampont, where Thurman's friend Florent lives, about 20 kilometers from Brévaq. They both boarded at the high school in Langres, a fortified city that dates back to Roman times and punches above its weight when it comes to education. I also know it to be one of the coldest places on earth, having watched Thurman play rugby there on a bone-chilling January afternoon.

Thurman and Florent both tested into *Sciences Po*, which in France is usually a prelude to a life in politics or public administration, if not high level banking or business leadership.

Their friendship is as tied to their shared disinterest in that traditional career path as to their having grown up together.

Florent works in his father's furniture manufacturing business, managing budgets and helping with business development. The plant itself is about the size of a football field, with industrial saws, wood presses, lacquering machines, and other equipment for making wood furniture.

It's almost noon when we arrive, and Florent's mother is preparing lunch at their house, which is on the same piece of land as the business.

Florent shakes my hand enthusiastically – he seems a little sheepish about being stuck in a town 10,000 miles away from the nearest big city.

He's mostly very proud to be working in the family business. He's applying whatever he learned from his classes in political science, and introducing design software and a bunch of other ideas that he hopes will allow the business to thrive in a more digital era – and perhaps survive his father's retirement.

He walks us through each room in the factory, explaining the processes, pointing out which machines are new, and how the wood is cut to make the most efficient use of the raw materials.

"My grandfather founded this company," he says proudly.

Like my own grandfather founded the company that boasts of being "family-owned and operated for more than 135 years." So this is what it really looks like, I think, when a business remains in one family's hands.

Florent's father climbs down the stairs from his mezzanine office overlooking the factory floor. He is a fit-looking middle aged man with curly gray hair and massive hands.

He shows Florent some drawings, and they stand shoulder to shoulder, speaking in low, respectful tones.

Florent's father, steeped in his own father's business, has probably never left the area, aside from during his military service. He is slightly older than me, and would have been a child during the culture wars that led France into the modern era of privately owned television stations and American chain stores, leaning indifferently on the doorpost of history and watching the world change in ways he didn't like very much.

Now, he has given Florent – young as he is, and inexperienced in the ways of the world – massive responsibilities. The fate of the family business is really in the younger man's hands.

The French tend to believe in their educational system, and someone who graduates with a degree from a prestigious school like *Sciences Po* is generally deemed worthy of trust. I wonder if I would have entrusted the Kupfer silk factory to Thurman at this age, if it had been mine to entrust. Perhaps if I knew him better, I think.

And then again, the French have a real social safety net. It lets you take chances.

Florent's father shakes Thurman's hand vigorously – they've known each other for years, too. He shakes mine limply while only glancing at me briefly.

I wonder if he knows what a poor father I have been to Thurman, or whether he's just inherently shy. My guess is he knows all about me, has heard about it through Florent during all those years of adolescent friendship, and he doesn't want to betray his profound sense of disgust with me.

I sense a milder but persistent level of scorn coming from Florent. I'm not used to this – Clara's friends hold me in fairly high regard. But then again, Clara didn't have to grow up without me, or make hollow-sounding excuses on my behalf that she probably didn't even believe herself.

Florent invites us for lunch, but Thurman explains that he has to be at his mother's by one p.m. There's no telling how she'd react if he happened to be late.

As we pull away, a half-dozen cardboard boxes full of books and clothes changing the center of gravity in the back, I feel a lurch of regret that I won't be leaving Thurman anything as substantial as a furniture business. I can't help wondering about the Hirschkind family business in Ansbach that could have been mine.

"It isn't much farther," I say, as if Thurman didn't know.

The road is flat, the countryside lush and unremarkable. There are traffic circles at every intersection, as if the local politicians factored in a population boom that never came to be.

As we near Brigitte's house, Thurman and I start joking about different scenarios that might unfold during his exfiltration. She might be waiting for him with a butcher knife, squatting in a corner of the kitchen. "Come in," she would say when he knocked, then charge at him with the knife held like a bayonet, screaming, "I'll never let you get away! Never! I gave you the best years of my life!"

Those would be the words of a scorned wife – not a mother. But it wouldn't be uncharacteristic of her.

"Or she could hold the knife to her own throat," Thurman says, laughing. "And threaten to kill herself if I leave!"

We get to Brévaq, the small village where he grew up. We drive past the school, which still looks modern but has been there for at least 30 years. I guess it was new once. We pass the café at the town's main intersection, which is where I'm going to wait for Thurman after I've dropped him off.

We get to the house, the former water mill. It's concrete, cylindrical, foreboding, and set back from the road some 25 yards. I park to the side, hoping Brigitte doesn't see the car – or who is driving it. I think maybe a curtain moves, although it could just be the wind.

"What if she asks you who drove you here?" I ask.

"I'll just tell her it doesn't matter, they're not coming into the house either way. But I'm just worried she won't talk to me at all, that she'll just ignore me while I pack my boxes."

His lower lip trembles and I see the little boy who used to cry for her every night that he spent in my custody, wondering why she didn't love him enough to rescue him from my rough indifference. I see him steeling himself for an act he only half wants to commit. I want to comfort him and tell him that she loves him more than he realizes, but I don't want to give her that. And I don't honestly know if it's even true.

But it was she who made sure that he got his hands on every book on Napoleon ever written during the year he dreamed of enrolling in the French military academy. It was she who made sure he had a Mac Book Pro for high school, she who made sure he had a desk in a quiet part of the house so he could study without being distracted by the TV. Above all, it was she who made sure he understood that his mind was the most important field of honor, the most fertile field to plow, his surest bet in life.

Now, though, he had grown out of adorable childhood and into adulthood. He had joined the ranks of "the others," people who would inevitably disappoint her. She told him to bring his own cardboard boxes, making it clear she wouldn't help him at all – that he is on his own.

His eyes well up.

I put my hand on his shoulder and give it a squeeze. "Text me when you're ready," I say.

He hops out of the truck lightly, opens the hatch and pulls out a stack of folded cardboard boxes and a roll of translucent packing tape.

I turn the truck around and head back to the café, where I park and sit on the patio outside the front door.

This isn't Paris. No one is around, it's the quiet part of the noon lunch break, when people are digesting and slowly getting ready for the rest of the day. There will be a mid-afternoon coffee break, maybe a beer. A few more hours of work and then back in their cars or trucks, a stop at the local café for a drink, and then home for dinner and the kids.

No one comes out to serve me, so I walk inside, where the owner is cleaning a few glasses behind the bar. I ask if she's still serving lunch. "Sorry, you're too late," she says.

She's in her early fifties, wearing brown, calf-length boots, a tight blouse, and jeans. Her blonde hair is in a ponytail. I play with the idea of moving here, settling down with her, helping her run her little country café, which probably only does enough business to support one adult.

I order an Orangina and go back outside. I check my phone for a text message, but of course it's too soon for that.

There's an urgent text from Bette, however. *Gypsy got bit by an animal and I need to take her to the vet, but I need $8 for gas and $27 for the vet. Can you help me out?*

There's an app for that, and I send her the money.

I check my work email and find one from my Parisian colleague Sebastian, who is providing more business cover for my time in Europe. There's a customer event at Longchamps, the famous horse racing track that was once the flavor of the "tout Paris," as popular as the heavyweight fights featuring Jack Johnson – the first Black man to ever win the heavyweight title (oh, let's say it – the first Black man allowed to fight for it, the first to hold it, the first to get arrested and jailed for it) – whose skin color and power and speed delighted such turn-of-the-century artists as Sonia Delaunay, Colette, and Apollinaire.

I am familiar with this history because my friend Claude Meunier wrote a book while I still lived in France that tied together many things about Paris and France that I hold dear.

Mine is not the Paris my mother knew – the Paris of Nazi collaboration, of Russian emigres escaping Soviet Bolshevism and Russian pogroms, nor is it the other Paris my mother romanticized – the Paris of the painters and the poets, of the actors Louis Jouvet and Jean Gabin.

Mine is the Paris of James Baldwin and Richard Wright, and Norman Loftus, the Black writer 20 years my senior who rented me a room while I was in college and then become a friend.

Norman was wily enough to landlord his way to owning apartments in Manhattan, the Hamptons, and Paris, all on a college professor's salary. How he accomplished this in racist America is anyone's guess. He once told me he loved being in Paris most of all because here, he was just a man, not a Black man.

The book my friend Claude wrote about Black American boxers in Paris is itself a compendium of everything beautiful and admirable about the French – their ability to recognize and celebrate beauty in its myriad forms, and their appetite for every sensual pleasure under the sun, from the arts, to sex, to fast cars, to athletic achievement.

There are times I still see that Paris, stuck in an interstice between modern and post-modern, a relic sharing a shelf with other knick-knacks, a Paris as old as old Rabelais or Molière or Stendhal. The Paris depicted by Degas and Manet and Cézanne, walked over by Hemingway and F. Scott Fitzgerald and James Baldwin.

I love the still-old places tucked away, the surviving ateliers in the Bastille, the untouchable monuments, and the proud old places like the Longchamps racetrack.

I check my phone again – still nothing from Thurman.

The café owner comes out and says she's got some bread left over from lunch. "Would you like a sandwich?" she asks.

"With pleasure. Is there enough for two sandwiches? My son won't have had anything to eat either," I say.

"Sure. Salami and butter okay?"

I nod and smile my thanks.

When she brings them out, I snarf mine down and resist eating the other one.

A guy drives up to the café in a beat-up white Peugeot sedan, the undercarriage rusted out around the wheel wells, the transmission belt squeaking. He's got a country-music beard, dark hair, cut-off jean shorts, high-top Converse sneakers, and sunglasses. He's tall and rangy, and he looks tough.

It occurs to me that maybe Brigitte did see me out the window, did figure out who was driving Thurman. Maybe he's her lover, maybe she's asked him to fuck me up – all she has to do is tell him what a bad father I've been, and how I was lousy to her when we were together. I wait for the collision as he walks in my direction.

He walks towards but then past me and into the bar, which doubles as a *Tabac*. So maybe not.

He comes out a few minutes later with a pack of cigarettes. He looks at me, tapping the pack against his thigh and weighing his options. He turns to me. "You're Thurman's father?"

"Yes," I say. "How do you know?"

"Brigitte told me."

"Okay," I say.

"You're a right bastard."

"I don't know about that," I say.

He glares at me for an eternity-and-a-half.

I point at an empty chair at my table. "Would you like to take a seat?"

He walks over and puts both hands on the back of the chair, and for a moment I think he's going to pick it up and swing it at me. He's probably considering the same option, but he thinks better of it. He walks around and sits.

He opens his new pack of cigarettes and offers me one, an automatic gesture which I accept.

"So you're with Brigitte?" I ask.

"Yeah. In a manner of speaking," he says.

I know what he means, but I also know better than to say anything to that effect. Being her lover is a precarious proposition at best. When you factor in all her moods, her sudden about-faces, her demands – not for material things, but for absolute spiritual purity – it's a full-time job managing her expectations.

"Well, I know she's probably said a lot of terrible things about me, and some of them are probably true. But I'm not as much of a bastard as maybe you think."

"You left her, you left your own son behind and flew halfway around the world. The poor kid didn't have a dad," he says, trying to rile himself up.

"Have you ever had an ex? Do you think everything she says about you is true, especially later, to other men?"

"Yeah, but you left her high and dry."

Left her high and dry.

A right bastard.

His words bounce around my head like bingo balls that spell out the word guilty.

I've already explained myself to Thurman, and he says he's accepted my rationale. But I wonder.

Shortly after he was born, as Brigitte was pushing his stroller down the rue Faubourg Saint Antoine, we saw a billboard advertisement for men's underwear that featured a naked, blond model with full red lips and pert little breasts with pink areola.

"Do you think she's pretty?" Brigitte asked.

It was a trap question if ever there was one, but we had sworn to be absolutely honest and authentic with one another.

"Sure," I said. "In that classic-model sort of way."

Silence ensued.

"What?" I asked.

"Nothing."

"Tell me."

A deep, dramatic sigh. "If you're attracted to that commonplace sort of beauty, we clearly don't belong together."

We fought about the absurdity of fighting about this.

"You're a fucking self-absorbed lunatic," I shouted, kind of like a lunatic myself.

"We're done," she said. *Fini.*

I begged her to take me back. I swore I didn't like that sort of woman and never had, that I only wanted her hard edges and her idyllic sex, nothing like the temptations offered by this vacuous, cynical, run-of-the-mill, two-dimensional floozy plastered on a Parisian wall. I swore I would never shout at her again, at least not in front of the kid.

No, she said. It is over.

We had never married, and now, we didn't go before a judge, never went through any official channels when it came to settling typical custody and child support stuff. She said, "we can settle this like civilized people."

I should have listened to Claude, who said, "it's because we're civilized people that we use the courts."

Instead, Brigitte and I battled constantly over who would have Thurman, and when. If there was an art fair in Barcelona, she would drop Thurman off with me unannounced. She might not be home when I dropped him off at the agreed time, and he and I would have to cool our heels at a neighborhood bistro, his overnight bag on the seat next to mine, his stuffed koala bear in his little clutches, asking from time to time where his mommy was.

Thurman was three.

It wasn't just she who was distracted, and whose attention was drawn to other, more pressing concerns. Whenever I was stuck in Paris with Thurman, I would yearn to be back with Liz, Clara's mom. Liz had opened an American-style diner in the small Atlantic-coast town of La Rochelle (pop. 15,457), popular among wealthy Parisians and other European hobnobers, its sea port filled with the elegant white sails of yachts and other pleasure boats. Its medieval towers were untouched by Allied bombing during WWII because, uniquely among French Atlantic seaports, its harbor was too shallow for military purposes.

Liz was financially well-off, at least enough to capitalize a brand-spanking new restaurant, and I thought that for once I wouldn't be the main bread-winner in a relationship. I wouldn't have to be the emotional and financial rock.

I met Liz through her mother, another writer represented by the same agent as I. She and her mother came to France to hear from me what it was like living in France, and I met them again about a year later, this time while I was visiting friends in New York.

Brigitte and I had been separated for several months, and Liz and I went from zero to 60. We became a couple and agreed to open the restaurant together, with me as the official face of the business. The arrangement made sense because I was the one with official status in France, I was fluent in French, and, as a man in a phallocentric society, had an easier time conducting business.

I was someone with whom she wouldn't have to navigate a culture gap, but who was also familiar enough with French culture to help her with the actual business end of things – negotiating with suppliers and bureaucrats, talking to customers, and managing staff.

Not that she was deliberately transactional or conniving about this – it was lust at first sight for both of us. She loved sex, and at first, I don't think she wanted anything more than a fling. She loved sex for the sake of sex – love only came later, and then the idea of working together on this business.

She moved into the apartment I had rented just outside Paris, close to where Thurman lived with Brigitte, and we spent a few months locating the right place for our eatery. Once we found it, we spent a few more months on the closing, and then renovations. It was no mean feat transforming the space from traditional, fussy French to modern, open, American.

Liz was the opposite of Brigitte – even-tempered, rational, unartistic, dark-haired, sporty, and purposeful. With her, I didn't feel any pressure to conform to some idealized version of who I was. We fell in love. I promised myself to watch the short fuse I was becoming aware of having.

My watchfulness didn't last very long.

We were days away from our opening day. Liz and I were floating on adrenaline, and I was doing side work, making sure ketchup bottles were clean and salt and pepper shakers were set up properly on each table.

Liz noticed the shakers weren't all full.

"Who cares?" I said.

"They need to be full at the start of every shift."

"How come?"

"That's just the way it's done," she said.

Something about being contradicted, or having to start the work over, of having my flow interrupted, made me snap.

"Oh, for fuck's sake," I shouted. I swiped at the shakers I was working on, sending them clattering and shattering onto the black-and-white floor tiles. I stormed out the door and down the street, to the port where the fancy ships bobbed on the wake of richly bedecked yachts.

An hour later, I slunk back to the restaurant and apologized.

"What the hell is wrong with you?" Liz asked quietly.

I honestly had no idea.

And then came Clara.

Liz gave birth in La Rochelle, and the experience left her alienated from France: the callous nurses seemed unfeeling with their rigid English, the home aides sent by the French administration seemed more judgmental than helpful, and the ladies at the day care center were wedded to modern child-rearing principles, such as letting a baby "cry it out," at the expense of catering to a mother's maternal instincts.

"Clara shouldn't grow up here," Liz said. "These people suck."

There wasn't room to disagree. It was a matter of whether or not I was on board. And would I bring Thurman with me if I came?

I'd like to think – and so I've told Thurman – that I didn't have a choice. That I had to leave or else lose Clara. And I didn't want to lose Clara; I didn't want to turn back into one of those single dads watching his kid at the playground, a pathetic loser who only gets to see his kid on someone else's terms, on someone else's turf, by someone else's say-so.

France was full of single mothers, many of them hoping to meet someone who would accept the package deal – the woman and her brood. Their ideal mate was someone who also had a kid with someone else – someone who understood the challenges, the forced compromises, the underlying mix of affection and grievance that characterizes divorced parenting.

Playing in that end of the pool was too depressing for words, and I had done it too often before meeting Liz. See how good I am with kids? I could be your baby-daddy too. Ugh.

Did I want to be a lonely American knocking about Paris with a kid caught between two cultures, having no chance of ever totally fitting into France, but away from the US too long to ever belong there either?

Liz and I talked about bringing Thurman to the US with us, but I never took that idea seriously. He would have been miserable without her, and if he now knows what a rotten mother she was, he would never have known it and would have resented me forever, had I spirited him away.

It wasn't a life-and-death kind of choice, it wasn't cataclysmic compared to what my mother and father had had to endure. But each of our problems are ours alone, and their magnitude isn't measured against any other backdrop than our own experience.

The last day that I saw him before we left for the US, Thurman was seven.

We were on the platform at the Gare de Lyon train station in Paris. I hugged him and reassured him that we would catch up on Skype every week, and that I would see him very often. It doesn't take much longer to fly from New York to Paris than to take the train from Paris to La Rochelle, I told him.

Not realizing that Brigitte would move him out of Paris, that she would block my Skype calls, or that she would do everything to blacken my name with him and drown our fledgling relationship in a sea of her bitter spittle.

Also not thinking through the reality that I wouldn't be able to afford flying round-trip to Paris more than once a year, instead of seeing him every month.

At the train station in Paris where I handed him off to my friend Philippe, who was then still seeing Brigitte, Thurman cried in my arms. Later that day, he called and cried on the phone because when he let her know that I was leaving, Brigitte punished him for my departure. I hadn't given her a heads up, fearing she'd stop me from seeing him again while I was still in France. I didn't imagine she'd take her anger out on him.

I cried too, and Liz suggested we snatch him on the way to the airport. But that wasn't going to happen, and even Liz knew that when she said it.

Maybe I should have stayed in France; maybe Clara would have been fine without a father, and I could have found myself a Magali or an Anne or a Celine, and Thurman could have continued a life of being shuttled from one angry, frustrated parent to another.

I don't have a way of redoing my own life, any more than I do of rewriting the history of post-war Europe. But given everything that happened, I realize I'm lucky to have the relationship with Thurman that I do.

———

Now I'm just sitting here waiting for this guy to make up his mind and either start throwing hands, or throw up his hands and walk away.

He snuffs out his cigarette in the ashtray, and I can see his shoulders tense. He flexes his arms, puts his hands together, extends his arms and cradles the joints of his fingers. He's trying to look tough, but I can tell it's mostly a front. Like me, like any sane person, he probably shies away from a fight unless he's cornered. Brigitte has cornered him, and I want to uncorner him.

"I left her, but not high and dry. She probably told you I never sent money – that's what she told Thurman too, when he was a kid. But when he turned 18 and he went to the bank and asked to see the statements, he saw it wasn't true."

The guy folds his arms, listening, weighing his options. I'm trying to simultaneously defuse but also dissuade. I've talked my way out of a couple of confrontations – part of what makes me a decent PR guy, I suppose.

I smile at him; I know that the more I can project calmness and confidence, the more likely he is to avoid a physical confrontation with me.

"Have you met Thurman?" I ask.

He shakes his head.

"I drove him here – he's packing up his stuff. You can go over there and ask him how he feels about me."

"I think I'll pass," he says.

"Let me buy you a drink," I say, maybe pushing my luck.

"Fuck off," he says.

He stands up. I'm not sure if he's leaving or about to throw down. His hand goes to the chair-back, and I'm wondering if I need to use that bottle of Orangina. My mind flashes back to a night many years ago, before I'd even met Brigitte, and I was with a woman named Sandrine who originally brought me to Paris and tutored me in modern French.

They say the best way to learn a new language is to sleep with your dictionary. In my case, I had learned French from my mother, but it was French from the 1930s, and Sandrine helped me update my argot.

One night, early morning really, sitting at the outdoor terrace of the Café des Artistes on the boulevard St. Germain, a couple of middle-aged French drunks started chatting her up as if I wasn't there. They pulled up a couple of chairs and started asking her if she had plans for later. They mistook my restraint for cowardice, and became aggressive, one of them putting a hand on her knee.

The anger I felt is still palpable, but most of the fight itself is a blur. I hit one of them with the flimsy bamboo café chair I had been sitting on, and pushed the other one to the floor. None of the waiters or other patrons came to break up the fight, and I hadn't hurt either one of them enough to scare them off. They regrouped on the pavement and seemed prepared to take another run at me. I picked up a water pitcher and smashed it against the side of the marble-topped café table, showing them the jagged glass.

They looked at one another and took off down the street.

"You're bleeding," Sandrine shrieked.

My hand was gushing blood.

We ended that night at the *Hôpital Hôtel-Dieu* where I got eight stitches at the base of my right thumb. Sandrine broke up with me soon after, and I always felt like something about that brawl had factored into the end of our relationship.

"Jean-Claude," the café owner calls out. She's standing in the doorway. "You're not making trouble, are you?"

He motions towards me and opens his mouth, then shuts it. "Ah, screw it," he says to nobody in particular. Then to me: "You're lucky, you know that?"

"Yes," I say, "I know."

He stomps off, gets in his car, guns his engine and peels off down the road.

"Don't mind Jean-Claude," the owner says. "He's always barking about something, but he's not a bad sort."

"I wasn't worried." I smile, lying my ass off.

I drive back to the mill, and text Thurman: *Are you okay?*

He responds a few minutes later: *Just finishing up.*

Ten minutes go by. Still no sign of Thurman. I grow anxious, wondering what she's putting him through. I decide not to tell him about my encounter with Jean-Claude.

Then I see Thurman walking away from the building with a stack of boxes in his arms. I stay in the car while he piles them into the back of the truck. He gets in and I hand him his sandwich.

"Thanks. I needed this," he says between giant bites.

There is nothing in Brévaq that inspires me to scatter my mother's ashes here. Maybe elsewhere, I think.

We drive back towards the highway in silence.

"How was it?" I ask finally.

"Good. She actually spoke to me. She kept asking me if I wanted something to drink, something to eat, if I needed help. So finally I said, 'is there something you want to say to me? If so, let's talk.' So that's what took so long."

"What did she say?"

"Just bullshit mainly. Like why am I freezing her out? What has she done to me? Why is the world abandoning her? I told her the world isn't abandoning her – she's the one doing the abandoning."

He sighs deeply, and I'm not sure if it's relief or an attempt to hold back tears. I try to appreciate how hard it must be to leave your mother, even if she's been a complete and useless wreck, a malignant force in your life.

He puts his hands on his knees, and I notice they are not so much trembling as fluttering, as if he was feeling new emotions. I do not allow myself to smile. It is a triumph I haven't earned.

For the first time since we arrived in France, he seems at peace. It's going to take much longer, of course, for him to get over the rejection from his mother. But for a moment – and maybe a moment he'll hang onto for longer and longer as time goes on – he understands something about himself. He understands that it's her and not him, that he's deserving of happiness.

He puts his hand on my shoulder. "Thanks for being here for me. This was an important moment in my life, and you were here."

"It's the least I could do," I say. "You know, she really did, she really does love you. She's just too sick to admit it."

He doesn't respond right away. "You paid for my teeth," he says. "That was very important to me. She wouldn't do it – she said the crooked teeth made me look like a cute little rabbit. She didn't love me enough to understand that I didn't want to go through life, go to university, looking like a cute little rabbit.

"If it hadn't been for you, I never would have had the nerve to ask Swan out on a date." His first girlfriend. "So thank you for that too. You were there for that too," he says.

"And then there's the advice I gave you for when you don't know what to say to a girl at a bar," I say.

"I actually used that once," he says, and we both crack up. I have to pull over on the shoulder of the road, I'm laughing so hard and tears are burning my eyes.

Thurman had once confided to me that he couldn't get up the nerve to talk to a girl he didn't know. I told him: "just walk up to her and say, 'you remind me of my dear old dad.'

"And when she inevitably asks how that is, you say, 'Because my dad said when I see a really attractive girl at a bar and I don't know how to start a conversation with her, I should just say, "you remind me of my dear old dad."

PHOTOS

Max Hirschkind in lederhosen along with his sister Beate, c. 1913.

*Beatrice Lutz née Hirschkind, the author's aunt, dressed as a flapper
in an undated photograph from the 1920s.*

*Max Hirschkind in a photograph from 1941, taken in Meillon and
pasted into the register of Jewish refugees kept by Mayor Paul Mirat.*

Hilde Hirschkind nee Bomeisl in a photo from 1941 taken in Meillon and pasted into the register of Jewish refugees kept by Mayor Paul Mirat.

Road sign indicating entrance to Meillon, located in the Basses-Pyrénées department (now known as the Pyrénées-Atlantiques).

Page of register kept by Paul Mirat, mayor of Meillon. Max Hischkind is one of the names on the page.

Paul Mirat, mayor of Meillon from 1935 to 1945, with cavalry Captain Bergès and Monsignor Auguste Daguzan, in a photo likely taken March 9, 1941. Photo taken by Max Hirschkind, the author's father.

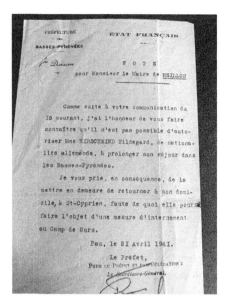

Letter from the prefect of the Basses-Pyrénées rejecting Hilde Hirschkind's application to remain at Mayor Mirat's house.

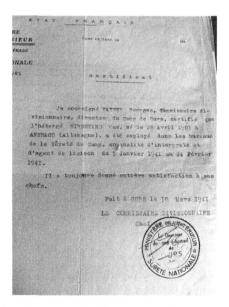

Letter from the director of the Gurs concentration camp attesting to Max Hirschkind's work as translator and interpreter.

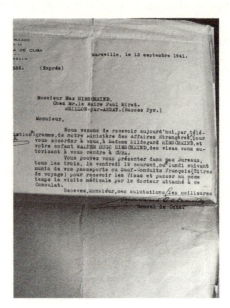

Letter from Cuban embassy in Marseille, addressed to Max Hirschkind care of Mayor Paul Mirat informing him that he, his wife and son have been granted entry visas to Cuba.

Gated entrance to the grounds of the Kupfer silk factory and residence, located at 15 Triesdorfer Str. in Ansbach, Germany.

Stolpersteine, or literally stumbling blocks, with names of former Jewish residents who were deported and, usually, exterminated in Nazi death camps.

Front view of entrance to Kupfer silk factory offices and residence.

Patrick Buron, current mayor of Meillon (l) and Paul Mirat, grandson of the former mayor, holding Mayor Mirat's register of foreign refugees. Behind them is a war memorial.

Paul Mirat, grandson of Mayor Paul Mirat, at the Paul Mirat exhibition center in Meillon, next to a portrait of his grandfather.

Max Hickins on holiday at the Catskills area inn Auberge des 4 Saisons, Shandaken, NY, c. 1965.

Undated photograph of Viviane Hickins nee Bronstein, taken in Queens, NY.

7

WHAT DID YOUR FATHER DO?

We arrive in Ansbach in the late afternoon. Thurman and Laura lean forward as I point to landmarks I've seen in guide books. We cross the Rezat, the small river represented on the city's coat of arms. (The town's coat of arms includes three little fish swimming in the Rezat. My father once joked that the village could only accommodate three fish – one of the few things I ever heard him say about his home town.)

I park at the hotel, which is across the street from a stone gate that sits where the original walls to the seventh-century burg must have been.

The carefully restored wall has columns on either side of the main gate, topped with stone heads of classical composers and Romantic poets sculpted to resemble Roman emperors. There is a horse-drawn carriage in the entryway of the hotel, to evoke the town's bucolic past. All these ornaments would seem ostentatious for a city, let alone a small hamlet in the hinterlands of Bavaria.

We pile out of the car and stretch our legs after the five-hour drive. I lift Max out of his car seat, the back of his shirt clingy with sweat, and I let him run up and down the carpeted stairs of our hotel.

We encounter a certain fussy formality from the front desk clerk, a dowdy young woman who justifies the high cost of the rooms by making us feel a little unwelcome. And we are faced with a logistical challenge – either the suitcases or the people can fit in the elevator, but not both. Thurman solves the dilemma by carrying our luggage up the stairs.

Suitcases safely in our stifling rooms, the majestic beds festooned high with pillows, and electrical outlets in short supply (how are we going to charge our phones, iPads, and power my CPAP?), we meet back up in the lobby.

Waiting for Thurman to come down from his room, Max entertains Laura and me by flirting from his stroller with the front desk clerk, whose chubby cheeks crease with pleasure at his attentions.

"Where are you from?" she asks, softening a little.

"New York," I say.

"Oh, we don't have a lot of visitors from America. We used to have an army base here of American soldiers, but there are fewer now."

We go outside, Thurman offering to push Max in his stroller over the bumpy cobblestones.

The town center has been turned into a pedestrian mall. The streets are narrow and the buildings, ancient. Exposed wood beams bulge from building facades to restrain the aging, crumbling stone walls they support.

There are a few typical retail chains – Sephora, H&M, C&A – but many more stores that are independently owned. Even a place called Chili's isn't part of the restaurant franchise.

I want to visit the Jewish cemetery that Google locates for us on Rügelandstrasse, but which we can't find and about which no one we ask seems to know anything about. It was as if I were asking for directions to the Martian cemetery.

It turns out that the cemetery was destroyed by vandals in 1950, and the graves moved to a secure location. The listing on Google Maps proves that some things don't have the right to be forgotten.

We stroll onwards towards Rosenbadstrasse, where the Ansbach synagogue still stands. It is no longer open, nor even possible to visit. It has a plain wall, yellow of course, with only a small plaque indicating that it was once a Jewish temple. A video camera is affixed to the wall above the door, angled to dissuade vandals.

The synagogue has a website that indicates that private tours can be arranged through an email address provided, but no one ever responded to the many attempts I made to contact them for a visit.

We get a table at a café across the street from the disaffected temple and order drinks. We allow Max to run around the cobblestoned plaza since there are no cars, but Laura watches him closely.

"Do you get a lot of Jewish visitors here to look at the synagogue?" I ask our waitress, a young woman dressed like a punk. You can see she'd like to be diffident and sardonic, but she's much too eager to please her customers to be a real renegade.

"No," she says. "Everyone knows there isn't much to look at."

"Well, at least it's still here. There aren't a lot of synagogues left in Germany."

"They only didn't burn it down because they were afraid the fire would spread to the other buildings," she says, shrugging.

"My father worshipped here," I say.

"Ah," she says as she walks away.

Thurman and I exchange a look of bewilderment.

"I guess she doesn't think anything of that," he says.

"Maybe she's embarrassed," Laura says.

"Maybe," I say.

"I don't see any sign of embarrassment," Thurman says.

We finish our drinks and keep moving, looking for a place to get dinner – and secretly, I'm hoping for an acknowledgement of my father's existence, even if I don't know what that would be. Here and there we walk over small square bronze plaques embedded in the cobblestones, scuffing them with our shoes. Upon closer inspection, they seem to mark the place where Jews lived until they were taken away and murdered by the Nazis. People walk over them as if they were nothing, unremarkable to new generations of Bavarians who seem to be doing everything they can to forget that episode in their history.

In truth, I want to fall in love with this place. It is where my father was born. It is full of handsome, meaningful buildings and parks, just like many European cities.

These are the streets my father walked. There is the old café where he and other Jewish friends gathered in the afternoon to drink schnapps, taste delectable sweets, and remake the world with their idealism. Here is where the margraves lived, and the theater, and the carefully preserved buildings on Martinlutherplatz, where my father and aunt met with friends, sat in cafés, made business deals. And here is the Hofgarten, where the posh bourgeoisie strolled on sunny afternoons wearing bowler hats and dueling scars.

I remind myself that the Germans are different now, and no one here today was alive, let alone responsible for what happened to my family in the 1930s and 40s. I don't want to look around resentfully.

As a child, in the developing womb of my own being, I disagreed with my father's every word – even as his words etched themselves like the truth on a stone tablet. He was a pessimist, a recluse, a misanthrope disguised as a hale fellow, well-met. His motto: You do what you must to survive. Pretend you like your neighbors – pretend so effectively that they open their arms in friendship.

But don't trust them. Don't tell them about your religion, or your political affiliations. Don't wear anything on your shirt that can serve as a target for a sniper. Don't kick bags on the sidewalk because they may contain bombs. Don't trust women who are too easy. Don't trust men who pretend to be your friend.

"When I was a boy," he once told me after I'd come home sobbing from a quarrel with my best friend Hal, "my best friend was a boy named Otto. But then he became my mortal enemy."

"How come?" I asked.

"He became a Nazi and he killed my mother," my father said. "So you see, friendship at your age means nothing."

I grew increasingly resentful of the old bastard because as far as he was concerned, nothing meant anything – not my friendships, not my love of baseball, and not my desire to hang around with my older sister Bette. As much as I also boiled with anger at this Otto, I knew that Hal would never try to kill me or my mother. I knew my father's story was something from another time, a time when people were pitted against one another for reasons that made no sense. I knew this was America. I knew no one would kill you for being a Jew or a Democrat or a Republican.

I look around me here in Ansbach, and I know that Otto is dead from old age or from battlefield wounds. Either way, he isn't here anymore. His children, if they still live in this town a half hour by car from Nuremberg, are probably fifteen years my senior, and his grandchildren are ambling out of a grocery store on their way home from work, not remotely responsible for my grandmother's death, and probably not wishing anyone dead at all.

But they live off the wealth that was created as much by Jews as by anyone else. Their health care benefits are funded by Hirschkind money! Their Autobahn was built with Hirschkind money! I feel this, and I also recognize the absurdity of these feelings.

And I can't shake the feeling that no one remembers. It's not history I want them to remember. No, I want them to remember my father, Max Hirschkind, and his mother, Dora Kupfer Hirschkind.

I want them to remember that they existed, that they lived here and loved here and made something of value here.

I want to love it here, but I'm growing to hate it.

In the morning, Thurman and I take Max to the Hofgarden, the park where my father must have played as a child. His namesake Max has been exceptionally cooperative, and I want to make sure he's had a chance to expend some energy before we get to the silk factory and our rightful ancestral home.

A five-minute walk from the hotel, the Hofgarden stands on 50 acres, and is a perfect place for strolling along gravel paths or spreading a blanket over the grass and having a picnic with your beloved. It has monuments to long-forgotten poets. There is a statue of Kaspar Hauser, the boy raised by wolves.

In other words, it's a wonderful place for adults to contemplate nature-in-a-box, but not really fun for little kids. There is a small playground hidden behind some tennis courts, but it is surprisingly poorly maintained, dirty, and empty. There are no other children for Max to play with.

"I'm anxious," I confess to Thurman.

"Of course, that's natural," he says. "I am too. Not really anxious – excited."

"Do you think there's a chance he won't show us the house after all?"

Thurman considers it. "There's a chance, but I doubt it."

I put my hands on his shoulders and shake him gently. "Don't you people know?? Max Hirschkind lived here!!" I shout.

Max runs over. "Am I going to live here?" he asks.

I smile, but I don't have an answer for him. "I don't think so," I say. "But who knows."

―――――

The Kupfer silk factory is on Triesdorferstrasse, outside the city center. Here, the buildings are newer, the cobblestones paved over with asphalt and the sidewalks made out of plain cement. The population is more diverse – which is to say there are Arabs.

Along the way, we find a shawarma shop for lunch on Maximillianstrasse and sit outside in the shade. I'm tapping my foot and jiggling my leg.

Max eats a hot dog – we've taken to calling Germany "Sausageland." He knows that isn't really its name, and it makes him smile to be in on the joke, like a real grownup. The rest of us have roast lamb and eat quietly.

"Are you sure you want Max and I to go in there with you?" Laura asks. "He might be a handful."

"No, it's his heritage too," I say. "And yours."

―――――

Thurman is wearing a clean tee shirt with blue and white horizontal stripes, and a pair of slacks. I'm wearing my suit pants and a collared shirt. I want to show respect to Klaus Kalbkopf. Laura is wearing jeans as well, very presentable, very middle class, very respectful.

We walk uphill on Triesdorferstrasse, and I imagine my father walking up this same hill, perhaps without as many – or any – shops along the way. We pass under a train trestle and I guess that it was there when he lived here. No one told me anything – I have no way of knowing.

We pass a storefront belonging to Sammy West, "your number one coach in Germany for guitar and vocals." He dubs himself "The Artistmaker" and has a picture of himself dressed up like a young Garth Brooks, with a cowboy hat and a plaid shirt, looking forcefully towards the future.

I chuckle, knowing my father would have considered this neighbor as nothing more than a prostitute selling out his soul for the most convenient buck.

The next building is the one, No. 15, surrounded by a long brick wall, high wrought-iron gates, and a weathered bronze plate on the wall bearing the name of Kupfer. Through the gate, we can see the house itself, an elegant three-story Victorian building, and to the right of it, a plain, single-story building that is obviously the manufacturing facility.

Between the front gate and the house, a lush yard with flower beds and tall trees, probably a quarter of an acre all told.

Under the Kupfer sign are a pair of bronze doorbells; one for the business, Kupfer Nähseiden Fabrik, and one for the Kalbkopf family. "The general manager still lives there with his family."

His family.

Embedded in the sidewalk in front of the gate are the now-familiar bronze squares: my grandmother Dora Hirschkind, my aunt Beatrice Hirschkind, my father Max Hirschkind, my grandfather Edward Kupfer – and even one for my late brother Walter – with their dates of birth and, if known, when and where they died.

"The cement around them looks new," Thurman remarks. "They must have just put them in."

We're a few minutes early, so we continue walking along to the end of the wall, to the driveway that leads to the loading dock. I turn around and see on the sidewalk a tall, slender man in shirtsleeves waving at us, his arms beckoning us back towards him.

"Look, it's him," I say. "Let's go!"

He is wearing jeans and a casual button-down shirt, and a full head of hair. He grins at me through slightly disordered front teeth. We shake hands and look each other in the eyes warily. He shakes hands with Thurman and nods to Laura, and bends down stiffly to say hello to Max.

"Look, I wanted to show you," he says, proudly pointing to the bronze squares in the sidewalk. He reads each of the names aloud, and tells me who each person is – "that is your father's mother, that is your father. We didn't know about your brother – is he still alive?"

"He died a few years ago, from an illness," I say. I don't want to say which illness because I don't want him to judge – and I'm convinced he would judge. Everyone judges. He, least of all, has any right. No one has any right. The bile begins to rise in my throat. "This is Max Hirschkind, your father." Oh, really? You entitled son-of-a-bitch with your Hirschkind-funded healthcare system, your Hirschkind-funded retirement system, and your Hirschkind-built mansion where you can park your ass every night.

"Shall we go in?" he asks.

"The offices are here in the house, the first two floors. The last story is living quarters. The factory where we make the threads is through here."

Of course I want to visit the factory – the factory my grandfather built and that my father managed.

Max starts fussing in his stroller, and Laura tries to shush him, but the more she tries, the less he cooperates. Usually, I would step in, but this is one time I won't. I want to focus on only one thing.

Klaus leads us from one factory room to another. Thurman is by my side, with Laura and Max behind us.

The first room has metal exhaust pipes hanging from the ceiling, and on the floor stand dozens of plastic bins, some lime green and some bright yellow, filled with industrial-sized bobbins of thread. More bobbins are perched on hooks attached to an olive-green machine that spins them.

"Most of what we make isn't silk," Klaus says. "It's too hard, and all the manufacturers want cotton or nylon."

He shows us a room where threads are dyed and then heated to a billion degrees. "Some of these threads are refractory to ordinary dyes and treatments, we have to treat them separately," he says.

I try to pay close attention – as if this were mine, or would be some day. The word refractory stands out to me: like my father, or Max, or me. Stubborn. Some would say Teutonic. It's a perfect word for to him to use.

I ask questions like a reporter. "What caused the disruption in the market? Where are your major markets?" that sort of thing.

Then, how's business? "My father told me at one point this was the second largest silk thread company in the world. Some Italian company was first," I say.

My father never actually told me this, but my mother did in her later years, while using the thread from his antique sample case to darn her clothes.

"Why do you care?" she asked when I protested the use she was making of the thread.

"Because." Because what? Would I be following in my father's footsteps across the eastern steppes of Russia, Turkey, Greece and India? Would I be showing the wares of my family business, signing letters of intent, receiving letters of credit, signing off on bills of lading? Why did I care?

"There is a lot of competition," Klaus says. "It's a very tough market. But we have our niche, we often supply our larger competitors when they need to deliver on short notice, or a short run. We think we can keep this business running another 20 or 30 years," he says.

"Another 20 years?" I say, shocked at the timeframe. "Why not another 135?"

Klaus gives me a patronizing smile that infuriates me, and he doesn't deign to answer my question.

We have finished our tour of the factory and are standing on the first floor of the house itself, next to the staircase that leads up to the other offices and then to the managing director's apartment, where my father grew up and banged his head on the wall in frustration and thought about girls and read the Torah and maybe masturbated thinking about Rachael or Rebecca or one of those sexy Talmudic vixens.

Here is where he grew up, where he watched his father build a business the way Thurman's friend Florent watched his father build a business. There is a chasm between my generation and my father's, with Thurman, little Max, and I on one side, and my father and my grandfather Edward Kupfer on the other. Between us, the Nazis and the War. The chasm doesn't exist for Florent's family because it wasn't Jewish – it wasn't fractured by world-historical forces.

I keep peeking up the carpeted stairs, the transition from place of business to place of family. Family-owned for more than 135 years. I long to climb them, to barrel past Klaus and crash through the door of history that separates me from my family. And my rightful heritage. I wait for the right moment to ask.

"I've been here 25 years, the last 10 years as the managing director," says Klaus. "There are many people here who have been here as long. It's given us all a good living, but these days it's hard to get young people interested in this business."

My father could have done better. My father could have inspired young people to work here.

Standing at the entrance of the main office, Klaus is interrupted a few times by employees asking questions, each of which he considers carefully before answering quietly but authoritatively.

"How often do you travel? I know you were on a sales trip when I first emailed."

"Oh, not so often," he says. "Maybe 12 or 15 percent of the time."

I'm shocked the figure is so low. *No wonder you're losing market share*, I think. *Get off your lazy ass and sell some damn threads!*

"What did you father do, did you say he worked here?" Klaus asks.

My heart stops beating, I stop breathing. I clench my fists and unclench them. I am staggered by the idiocy, the impertinence, the careless heedlessness of the question.

"He owned this place," I say, forcing myself to smile.

"Ah," he says, nodding. "I know everything about this company that happened since the war. Before and during the war, I know nothing. I know we didn't make silk during the war, but I don't know what we did make.

"Reinhardt Lutz married Gertrude in 1947 and they had a girl in 1953, Renate. Reinhardt died in 1959, and Gertrude ran it until 1975. Then Renate took over and still owns it, but I am the managing director. She's no longer active."

Something suddenly seems off – a part of the story that doesn't jive with what I think I know to be true.

"What about the other daughters?" I ask.

"There are no other children," he says. "I'm sure of that much."

I scratch my head.

Max has meanwhile been building to a slow boil, and finally explodes, crying and demanding to be taken out of his stroller. Laura can't control him – no one can control him. Laura tries jollying him up, but to no avail. He wants out, and that's that. I wonder if he's affected by the vibe – something he can't identify or articulate, but which maybe pervades the atmosphere like the stink of his favorite stuffed skunk: some mixture of anxiety, anger, rage, and hypocrisy – Rageanopoxrisy. Laura takes him outside, to the garden with the wooden swing. I turn back to my host.

"My understanding is that Reinhardt divorced my aunt because Jews weren't allowed to own property after the 1936 Nuremberg laws," I say. "So they divorced and the family all gave him their shares in the business until things got back to normal, so to speak, at which point they would get remarried and everyone would get their shares back. But then, when the war ended, he told my aunt, 'sorry, I met someone else and got married, and we have a couple of kids.'"

Klaus shakes his head.

"No, I don't know anything about that story, but Renate is the only child they had, and Gertrude was his wife only in 1947."

"So why did they tell me that story?"

Klaus shakes his head again – the mysteries of dispossessed

Jewish families are beyond his understanding. I don't blame him there.

"You would have to ask Renate," he says.

He goes into his office and scribbles her address on a sticky note and hands it to me.

I'm becoming irate at his willful ignorance of everything "before the war." He is becoming aware of my rising anger, and it makes him confused and anxious to end the visit.

"Can we visit upstairs?" I ask.

He shakes his head in the negative.

"I'm sorry, these are my private apartments," he says. "We do not even lock the door."

He can tell that all I want to do is rush past him and up the stairs, to fling open the unlocked door to his – my – apartment. But for some reason I stick my hand out for him to shake instead, and for an equally mysterious reason, he takes it.

Then he turns on his heel and goes inside, leaving Thurman and me on the door step of the building, of my house. We are outside, still in the garden with the swing, next to a small narrow stone path leading to the front gate.

No one is rushing us out, so Laura takes a picture of the three Hickins boys in the front yard – Michael, Thurman, and Max – with their backs to the house. Our house. What should be our house. What could have been our house. What may yet be our house.

The photo shows me scowling, Thurman with arms crossed, and Max looking perplexed.

How bitterly I want to have seen that apartment. Of course there would be no marker that says Max Hirschkind slept here, no dents in the wall from where he threw a fist or banged his head, no dried semen, no 19th-century sheets, no slaps from his father's hand imprinted on his ghostly visage, no smells of his mother's cooking. There is nothing to see here, not even a single beam of his light remains.

Or perhaps there is. Maybe there's some sign of him, or a secret sign he left for me to discover one day, left behind on the day he fled, but before knowing he would decide to never return, before knowing

I would exist. Maybe there's a hidden metal box like my mother's, a fake wall that I alone would discover, explaining why he never demanded restitution from his brother-in-law Reinhardt, or why he and his mother waited so long before leaving – so long that it cost his mother Dora her life, whereas their relative Paul Kupfer fled safely to New York and lived to print business cards with his name on them. Maybe there is still more for me to discover, some long-lost message.

We stand on the sidewalk outside the gates, now closed, and I peer at the doorbells. The Kalbkopf family.

"This should be your house," Laura says, unwittingly channeling Clara.

"In another life," I say. "In a universe where my father returned to Ansbach after the war, somehow still met my mother, and I was born. Everything else the same, everything different, but me being me and owning this house."

I try to smile, but I can see by the look on Laura's face that I am failing.

Max demands to hold Laura's phone so he can look at the photo of the three of us on the lawn in the garden where he too, in another universe, would be trying to climb the tree or cut through the air on a makeshift swing tied to its branch.

"My father used to say that our trees, the trees in Upstate New York, were nothing compared to the size of the trees in Bavaria," I say.

My mother used to smile at my father's tree parochialism. The black-and-red Swee-Touch-Nee can full of her ashes is in the Volvo. I had considered asking Klaus if I could scatter the ashes somewhere in the garden, a way of reuniting my father and mother in a historical overexposure, superimposing the improbably younger girl in her future husband's former childhood garden; now, obviously, I'm not going to do that.

———

At dinner, Laura is on her phone. Thurman and I take turns entertaining Max. The restaurant we pick is very highly rated, but the garden dining area makes it okay to have Max along. I guess there's an unspoken rule that you can bring a fussy toddler to a 5-star restaurant as long as there is outdoor seating.

"You're very quiet, Dad," Thurman says.

I look up from the menu, realizing I haven't been reading it at all. I've been thinking of the impossible puzzle of what drove my father to do the things he did – or didn't do. And what he did and didn't tell me.

"They lost a lot," I say.

I'm still trying to defend him, as much from my own recriminations as those I'm sure Thurman has too.

"I mean, did you see that house? The garden? The sense of security it must have given them. That they had this place, a way of earning a living, and a place to sleep comfortably and raise a family. That they thought was theirs. Taken away. Just had to leave it behind."

"And where does that leave you?" Thurman says.

"Or you? Or Max? But they couldn't know that, they couldn't see into the future. They didn't know if they even had a future. They had to run; to survive. It's impossible to understand the toll that must have taken on them. My father and his wife, what did it do to their marriage? What did it do to little Walter's psyche? Did he go through life with the vague memory of some beautiful garden that once could have been his?"

Thurman shakes his head.

"They were sophisticated people, and they weren't children," he says. "I still don't understand why they didn't come back."

I sigh. I don't understand that either. Or why my father told me that Reinhardt Lutz had remarried well before he had, or that he had two children instead of just the one.

The menu has extensive notations on the local provenance of the food. It has footnotes indicating that an extra 20 cents will be charged to guests who insist on mustard for their sausage, and another 20 for every extra slice of artisanal bread.

While we're still eating, Max watching YouTube Kids on my phone, the owner of the restaurant and his wife appear in the garden, hunting rifles slung over their shoulders, and belts crammed with shotgun shells like characters from *The Last of the Mohicans*. They are a squat, middle aged couple out for a little walk in the evening, with murder on their minds. Hunters in the ordinary course of business.

After dinner, we walk around the town center, and we let Max push his own stroller until he tires of struggling against the cobblestones. He abandons it in the middle of the sidewalk and starts running hither and yon, getting underfoot of other pedestrians, pausing at café terraces to gawp at the customers, shrieking and laughing his head off.

He might bother some people – in any case, I am hoping so.

Thurman hugs me at one point, puts his arm around my shoulder and commiserates wordlessly and probably on another wavelength.

"Thank you for including me," he says. "This is very important to me."

Thurman, for all intents a motherless man-child, connected finally to some kind of family history, if only one that has been sundered and fractured and is full of lies and deception. I am torn between anger and confusion. I am at a loss to understand what happened between my father, my aunt, and Reinhardt Lutz. Why, if Reinhardt didn't have any children, did my father and aunt just leave him the factory and the house?

When we get back to the hotel, we all sit in the lobby together. Suddenly, Laura holds her phone towards me. I can see it's an article written in German, apparently by some amateur historians, and it appears to be about a family named Hirschkind.

"Hirschkind is a pretty common name," I say, handing her back the phone.

"Are they all from Ansbach and have a grandfather named Eduard who owned a silk factory?" she says.

I snatch the phone back and scan the article for names I recognize.

We run the article through Google translate, which produces a mostly garbled English version that essentially explains that most of the Hirschkind family decamped to Wiesbaden in 1934, two years after the death of my father's father, Hugo. There are other names, but I can't imagine who those other people could be.

My father and sister meanwhile remained behind in Ansbach, to run the factory until they passed it on to Beatrice's husband Reinhardt.

After Germany invaded Poland and France, Max took his wife and son to Wiesbaden, and Beatrice divorced Reinhardt.

"No one ever mentioned Wiesbaden to me," I mutter. Yet another discovery.

There's some more information about Max, his wife Hilde and their infant son Walter, but the translation is unintelligible.

The article is signed by a couple of guys named Klaus Flick and Georg Schneider, writing under the aegis of the Wiesbaden historical society. It is clear they know a lot about my family, and have access to a lot of primary source material.

Thurman has been studying an online map. "Wiesbaden is only two hours to the north," he says. "We can take a detour to Wiesbaden on our way from Prague back to Paris."

I write to Drs. Flick and Schneider. I'm still fueled by my anger at Klaus Kalbkopf, but also by curiosity. Just today I've learned that the story of Reinhardt Lutz is different from what I had been told, and now I'm learning about Wiesbaden. Why Wiesbaden?

"Perhaps I could fill in a few gaps for you," I write, audaciously. I suspect they know much more about my family's history than I do.

8

YOU HAVE NICE SHOES!

All these people left behind. When Abo Bronstein, my mother's father, was forced to emigrate from Russia, he brought with him his second wife, Victoria, and their children Vivi and Georges, but left behind Victor, the son from his first marriage.

My mother abandoned her sons Chris and Johnnie to foster homes. My sister Bette lost her children in a custody fight. Camille did the same.

I abandoned Thurman to his crazy mother in the hinterlands of France.

Thurman once wrote to me, "What civil war, what natural disaster, what plague or Act of God forced you to leave me behind?"

No answer I could give would have been adequate. Without knowing, he had checked off a list of circumstances that had affected our family, but not me – at least not directly. A cascade in descending order of compelling determinants. For Abo, certainly *force majeure*. For Vivi, a barely excusable collection of extenuating circumstances. Me, I am inexcusable.

How do you move forward, though? My maternal grandfather Abo had little for which to reproach himself. My mother forgave herself too easily. But not forgiving yourself at all is the best way of passing the behavior down to future generations. I may be inexcusable, but I have to forgive myself for the sake of my children. At least that's what I tell myself.

I'm blasting the car eastward down the autobahn, trying to get out of Sausageland as quickly as possible.

I stop at the first rest area in the Czech Republic so Thurman can go to the bathroom.

"It feels so strange that I can't even pronounce the words on the road signs," I say to Laura. "In Germany I couldn't understand most of the words but at least I could pronounce them in my head. It was comforting somehow."

"*Ausfahrt*," she says, and we giggle.

It feels like the first intimate moment we've shared in days. Maybe weeks.

"Thanks for finding those guys in Wiesbaden," I say.

"Have they answered?"

"I haven't checked," I say. I go to look at my email, but instead find a text message from Bette: *Hey kiddo, I need five bucks for a new sparkplug and like 25 for some food at Walmart and Gene, the guy at the Straight Talk place said I can have unlimited text and voice for $39. Can you lend me the money, I'll pay you back.*

I send her $75.

I have seen nothing of Costa Rica, Venezuela, Nicaragua, and Panama – all places my father visited often on business, and from where he would bring me toys and guayaberas like the ones he wore in the summer.

But now I am in the Czech Republic, where he never went. It is the heart of Eastern Europe, post-Soviet, post-Western consensus. It came to the West too late for a true middle class to arise and prosper, so it is stuck between a past of privation and a future of privatization – in other words, privatized privation as opposed to state-run privation.

The view from the road outside Prague is unlike anything I have ever seen, a landscape of industrial detritus with none of the triumphs of the consumer society we so love and cherish. There are no big box stores, restaurant chains, or housing for the poor visible from the road. Where there is countryside, it is dark and leafless, as if the trees were too indigent to germinate, and the ground too barren to inspire color.

We arrive in Prague, and the GPS sends us through a series of tunnels that are nine miles long, under incandescent lights that turn everything yellow, including our skin; when we get to the other side, we are close to the historic old center, and the buildings hulk dimly in the fading light.

For now, we are in the real Prague, the Prague on the other side of the Old World-historical tracks. It is poor and grimy and unromantic. I resent it for not being Wiesbaden. I'm still waiting to hear from the historians, although I don't know if they're free or even want to see me. I feel the farther I am from Wiesbaden, the less I'm likely to see them.

It is late, Max is tired but wired and ready for action, and I am afraid this will turn into a depressing fiasco.

I park in front of the hotel, which is a few yards away from a commuter rail station and a busy commercial intersection. The lobby is brightly lit and the clerks speak English, and explain where to park the car – a garage two blocks away, closed off from the street by a huge iron gate that requires two-factor authentication – my magnetic room key as well as a passcode.

Laura and Max bring out bags up to our the room, while Thurman and I walk back to the hotel from the garage. For Thurman, this is thrilling. The streets are paved with adventure and possibility. For my part, I only hope the beds are comfortable but not too soft. It feels like a demilitarized zone, a penumbra between the old town and the workaday city. It is no-place.

Thurman has the pull-out couch; Laura, Max and I have a bedroom with an extra cot next to the bed.

"I miss that thing," I whisper to Laura. "You know, when you used to say, 'what you do to me!' Or when you hung over the back of my chair while was typing in the early morning in our old apartment on 95th street, and your hands would work their way around my chest."

She sighs, turns on her side to face me. "That's not coming back," she whispers back. "I'm not saying I'm never going to want to have sex with you anymore, but that feeling, that new excitement, it's not coming back." She pauses. "I'm sorry, that sounded harsher than I meant," she says.

"No, it's good. Thank you. I guess I can move on then, I mean move on from waiting for it."

"I'm not trying to hurt your feelings," she says. "I just want to be real here. I can't fake the excitement of novelty."

I really am grateful for her honesty, but also overwhelmed with grief. We have lost the novelty of each other's glow, and I have not replaced it for her with anything worth loving. All I've given her is temper tantrums.

In the morning, Thurman and I take Max to a park near the hotel. Thurman pushes Max's stroller, occasionally breaking into a mad dash and then coming to a screeching stop, causing Max to laugh uproariously.

The playground is situated in real Prague – the sector where people ride the tram to work, find solace in small cafés, and hope for companionship at places like *Single Bar* (the logo for which includes the intertwined symbols for Venus and Mars, in case anyone needed it spelled out).

The sidewalks and pavement are worn down, but clean.

I think about what it would be like to live here (as I do everywhere I travel), and I think it would be horrible, trapped between a carefully preserved ancient history and a lackluster modernity. I wonder how different life would seem if the only point of living were in the hope that things get better for your grandchildren; to have hope for the future instead of dreading it.

My interest in Czech history is limited, in part because the Nazi invasion seems like a sideshow to the events in Poland and France, and in part because I have no interest in revising my flawed world-historical perspective.

Part of me still idealizes Communism as a more humane system of government than what we have now. I don't want to think about the eastern bloc, or the gray skies of winter that permeate the soul of former Soviet satellite countries. I don't want to think about Tito or Stalin or Svaboda.

Of Prague, I know of Vaclav Havel and Franz Kafka. I know of the Velvet Revolution. Of Svabodas, I know only Ron Swaboda, hero of the 1969 World Series.

At the playground, a uniformed sanitation worker is picking up litter. Parents cluster with familiar faces, while Thurman and I sit on a bench, apart from the other adults.

"I don't remember mom taking me to a playground," Thurman says.

"Do you remember the time I took you to the one on *rue des Pyrénées* after work one day, and I fell asleep on the bench?"

He gawks at me and then laughs. "No!"

"It's true. One of the mothers pushed me awake. 'Is that your son?' she asked. 'He almost ran into the street!' I didn't believe her because you were still in the sandbox, but still."

"Yeah, but still!" Thurman says. He grins. "I forgive you."

"Thanks."

"If she were dead, at least I'd understand why she doesn't answer when I call her. But she's not dead, and I have to ask myself, what did I do that was so bad I don't deserve my mother's love."

I feel sick to my stomach.

"It's not you," I say. "It's her – her illness."

"I know that, but it's one thing to say it, and another to know it."

We sit back in silence, watching Max run from one play-scape to another, finding himself ever more challenging rope ladders to climb.

Eventually he finds himself at the water spout, holding the button DOWN so the little girls can fill their pails with water. There is no language barrier to his popularity with other kids.

"If history is any guide, he will lose his comfort level with girls just when he needs it most."

Thurman laughs knowingly.

Max loses one of his clogs, a bright pair of yellow Crocs with the friendly, grinning face of one of the popular Minions cartoons. One of the mothers picks it up and, smiling, brings it to me. The goofy, smiling yellow face seems to bring joy across schisms of generations, language, and culture.

We eventually pry Max away from the playground and meet Laura in the hotel lobby. Then we head to the historic center, which is only a few minutes away by foot. But the difference between the modern center and the old is staggering. The modern center looks like hardscrabble late 20th-century grimy. The old town, on the other hand, is small white paving stones, fairy tale castles, spiral church towers, buildings with uneven doorways, meandering streets through which the blood of history still runs.

We get to Republic Square, a large central plaza surrounded by high-end boutiques, cafés, and restaurants. We stop to let Max listen to an older man play a well-used violin. The man hasn't shaved in a couple of days, and his pants are worn thin at the knees, and ragged at the cuffs. Yet he has the dignity of a well-trained musician, his notes firm and clear, as if to insist there exists some higher state of being. When he's done playing an old tune, I give Max a few hefty yellow coins for him to hand to the musician.

Max approaches him tentatively, unsure of how to proceed. The man holds out his hand, takes the coins, and then holds the violin out for Max to touch. He shows Max how to pluck the strings, and smiles as Max coaxes some sounds out of the instrument. The musician kneels down and says, "You will have a lot of opportunities in life, you must take advantage of them."

I find my eyes welling up with tears, and I thank the man. I don't dare say it aloud, but I'm worried about the future that awaits Max, and I hope the man's words are prophetic – that Max does have a lot of opportunities, and not a world broken by my generation's greed, apathy, and ignorance.

"You have nice shoes!" he says, pointing to Max's yellow Crocs.

———

After lunch, we head towards the Vltava River, which cuts the city in half, and around which Prague grew into a great center of commerce and arts. Sweating through our shirts in the summer heat, we meander through the old cathedral plaza, which is filled with oddball circus and musical acts, and people in giant Panda suits that Max wants to touch.

"Imagine being inside that suit all afternoon," Laura says.

Then we follow the pubic curlicues of streets and alleys, admiring the audacity of colors, of hues, of a sky that beams under this, its favored offspring, the prodigal son of middle Europe.

It depresses me to think that its beauty is the work of people who later killed my people.

We – and a seeming billion other humans – cross the famous Charles Bridge, which is 1700 feet long, and lined with 70 statues of Christian saints. The climb is arduous, the view stupendous as we glimpse at Prague Castle in the distance. I take Max out of his stroller and hoist him onto my shoulders so he can enjoy the views.

Once on the other side, we find a small café and guzzle as much water as we can buy.

Laura wants to visit the old Jewish quarter, but the thought of going there depresses me. I'm tired of being reminded of the ramshackle existence my people suffered, the shabby quarters they were forced to live in, the scapegoating and the occasional tolerance to which they meekly submitted, lamblike and stubborn.

"I'd rather see Wenceslas Square," I say.

"That's a long way from here," Laura says, as if I can't read a fucking map. (I can't, but that's beside the point.)

Then I notice that Max is missing one of his clogs.

We retrace our last steps, but it's nowhere to be seen.

"That's okay, I have a pair of sneakers in the back of the stroller," Laura says.

"He loves those clogs," I say.

What I mean is that I love those clogs. I feel a sense of loss that is incommensurate with the actual loss of the footwear. Thurman, pushing the stroller, and Laura, have arrived at a busy intersection.

"You guys keep going, I'm going to look for the shoe," I say as they cross and I let the light change against me. A stream of tour busses block their view of me.

I turn quickly and walk back towards the bridge, leaving Laura, Thurman, and Max on their journey to the Jewish Quarter.

I have a heavy heart, feeling unreasonably depressed as I scan the sidewalk and the gutters for the single yellow clog. I work my way backwards across the bridge, telling myself he surely lost it when I put him on my shoulders.

I walk past the circus performers, the watercolorists, the impressionists, the mimes, the vendors of hats and pendants and wooden toys, past the clumps of Japanese tourists and the loud streams of German and American tourists following the green or blue flapping flag of the tour guide.

I check the garbage cans and the gutters and the lampposts and the tables and chairs of the vendors. Everything that is for sale is a reminder of what we cannot actually buy. Mementos are reminders of our noble, exalted feelings in the face of our inadequacy in the face of history. What would I tell myself looking at a refrigerator magnet of the Prague Castle five years from now? That I once visited a place where people lived and thought and created and died, and that some of them believed they were the same as me, just as others believed they were not like me, and sought to kill those that were like me and unlike them?

Having crossed the bridge, I retrace my steps further, pausing to think – did we pass this store? Ah yes, I remember the wax museum, I remember the Swarovski jewelry store, I remember the ice cream shop with the elf driving a horse and cart on the sidewalk. I scan the sides of the street and peek into garbage cans, hoping I'm not mistaken for a homeless person. I ask myself why – why am I ashamed of being seen as homeless?

I wind my way back to the restaurant where we had lunch and ask our waiter if he'd seen Max's yellow clog – the one he too had admired a few hours before. No dice.

I'm still wracked with an overwhelming sense of sadness for this missing clog, as if it were a puppy or a prized toy. It's just a shoe, I tell myself. I dash into a toy store and find a miniature Prague tram for

Max. I decide to buy everyone gifts, and I go back through the winding streets of Prague like the most precious of all tourists – the one hell-bent on buying something for everyone. For Thurman, a pencil and sketch pad; for Laura, a translation of "*It Is I Who Must Begin,*" a book of poetry by Vaclav Havel.

Now I hurry back to the street where our hotel is located, on the far side of Republic Square, proud of myself for not having got lost. I am somewhat happier now, but frustrated at the loss of the clog, and concerned that Laura and Thurman are worried about me.

I find them sitting outside at a café, waiting for me, as if they knew I'd get there soon enough; as if I hadn't left them in a fit of pique; as if nothing was wrong but that I had missed seeing the Jewish Quarter.

They are sitting catty-corner, Max napping in his stroller. There's something intimate about the way they're sitting – not in a sexual way, but as if their friendship had deepened in the last few hours.

"We were just talking about you," Thurman says.

"Oh?" I'm noncommittal.

"Good things," Thurman reassures me.

"Thurman was telling me about the time you visited him in... where was that?"

"Langres, the plateau of Langres where I played ruby."

"Yes, Langres. Am I saying that right?"

Thurman nods, and I resist the temptation to correct her slightly imprecise pronunciation.

"It was sleeting and freezing and Thurman says you stood there for hours watching a game of rugby," she says.

"It was not even a game. It was a practice, a night practice. Then the next morning a game, also the cold rain. It is known as the coldest place in France," he adds.

"And you coach a girl's rugby team. I like that – a feminist!"

"Surely," Thurman says.

Laura looks at me with a great deal of tenderness. "You're a good father," she says.

After dinner, we take a bus to Wenceslas Square. It is huge, and I remark that it's as long as the Champs-Élysées and just as wide, brightly lit and teeming with people. It stretches three miles from the top of the hill to the center of the modern city. We walk up the steep hill to the statue of Wenceslas and turn back to look at the immensity of the boulevard and to marvel that it was filled with hundreds of thousands of people when the Czechs shook off the fetters of the Soviet Empire.

It makes me want to reaffirm my faith in people, our ability to force change peacefully.

We walk into a capitalist emporium and happily devour ice cream.

We walk back to our hotels, Max slumping forward, asleep in his stroller. I check my phone for messages.

I stop walking. "I have an email from the Wiesbaden historians," I say. "They've delayed their holidays so they can see us. They want to know how soon we can meet with them."

9

NEIN! NEIN! NEIN!

We arrive in Wiesbaden at around 9:30 p.m., after night has pulled its blanket over the listless eyes of this quiet town. Wiesbaden is a much bigger city than Ansbach, but the stores have been closed for hours and the streets are mostly deserted. My stomach growls.

"I hope the hotel is still open," I say.

"Are we still in Sausageland?" Max asks sleepily.

"Yes, we're back in Sausageland."

The amateur historian Klaus Flick has agreed to meet us at 10 o'clock the next morning.

We gather in the lounge and watch TV while we're waiting. Two hundred fifty North African refugees drowned off the coast of Italy after having been chased away by the Italian coast guard.

"Trump: 'America is Full,'" is the headline of the international edition of *The Wall Street Journal*.

I spot Klaus and his colleague Georg Schneider walking into the lobby. We shake hands. Klaus is in his late sixties, tall and slender, with short-cropped brown hair, a warm smile and shaky but passable

English. Georg is more than a decade older than his colleague, stooped over, shorter, with a sharp nose and chin.

"I'm so grateful you could come on such little time warning," Klaus says. "It really is important to us."

Georg nods. "My English is not very good," he says, waggling his hand and pursing his lips.

Klaus leads us outside. "We have a little itinerary," he says. "I hope you don't mind we planned."

"Not at all," I say, smiling, as the four of us follow our guides. Just a few hundred yards from the hotel stands a large convex marble wall erected on a small, pedestrian island in the middle of the town center. It is some 18 feet high and twice as long, with two little slate-gray wings coming straight out as if to embrace the onlooker with a stony, remorseful elegance. It stands naked in the middle of a busy commercial street, bathed in a sunlight that is already becoming oppressive. It has little around it to protect its flanks or announce its arrival. It is just there.

Its surface is covered with hundreds and hundreds of slender stone nameplates, each engraved with the names of Jews rounded up in Wiesbaden in the early 1940s and sent to places like Sobibor, Treblinka, Izbica, Auschwitz, and Theresienstadt. Some of the camp names are familiar to me, others are not.

The memorial is stunning not just because of its size, but also because the countless nameplates are the names of Jews deported from Wiesbaden alone. Not countless. The memorial stands as somewhere between tragedy and statistic, a human-sized monument to inhumanity.

There are blank nameplates, Georg explains, to save room for newly discovered victims. Death had undone many in Wiesbaden, but they are still discovering more. "We many never learn how many," he says.

I start reading names silently, and Georg steps back a few feet, so as not to hover. He and Klaus stand by the curbside and wait. Waiting for me to find the names I am looking for, the names I'm dreading to find, the names I am blanking on. Suddenly, inexplicably, I am unable to remember my family name in the shadow of this monument to their memory. As if my own existence had been obnubilated by history.

Laura reaches me through the space-time continuum and calls me over to a section of the wall and points. There is the name. Hirschkind. Hirschkind, that's it! Dora Hirschkind née Kupfer.

Below Dora's nameplate is one for Lilly Hirschkind née Kupfer, and below that is one for Theobald Hirschkind.

I don't know who Lily and Theobald are, and I turn to Klaus helplessly.

"Your grandmother's sister and her husband Theo," he says.

"I never heard of them before," I confess. Georg's head snaps back almost imperceptibly. Klaus's eyes widen slightly.

They have questions, after years of following factual cul-de-sacs, years of grim and tireless research. But they have the courtesy and wisdom to respect my need for quietude. What Klaus and Georg don't realize yet is how little about my family I know myself, nor how much they will have to teach me.

Laura puts her hand on my arm, as if I needed steadying. Thurman comes over and hugs me. Klaus and Georg step closer to us, a subconscious gesture of shared humanity.

I feel confused. Who the hell are these people – and why didn't anyone tell me about them? "My grandmother's sister?" I ask.

"Yes," says Georg. "She moved here with her husband, in 1934. Your grandmother followed later, in 1938. Dora was deported in 1943. To Sobibor."

Sobibor. I had been told it was Auschwitz. Another in a series of false truths.

"Why here? Why Wiesbaden?"

Klaus coughs.

"Yes, good question," he says. "Why here. There was a large Jewish community here, well established for many years. Wiesbaden – you know what Baden is? It is a bath, how you say?"

"Like a kind of spa?"

126

"Yes, Wiesbaden was one of the first spas in Germany, in all this region, and it was owned by a Jew, Samuel Löwenherz. It was a town considered friendly to Jews."

"So they thought they would find refuge here?"

"Yes. Unfortunately, they were wrong," Georg says.

"Well, they would have been wrong anywhere in Germany. But they couldn't leave. Your grandmother tried to emigrate to Cuba, but she was refused permission to travel," Klaus says.

"Refused? Why?" Thurman asks.

"The Nazis wanted to take all her money," Georg says bluntly. "You'll see, later, what I mean."

I walk closer to the wall, wishing to be alone with my grandmother and my new acquaintances, Lilly and Theo, but I cannot find them again, reason having again abandoned me and taken my comprehension of the alphabet along with it.

There are things I will never understand, and questions for which I will never find absolute answers. Here is one of them: why didn't any one of my parents ever mention Lily and Theo? Not my father, perhaps because of the trauma, and not my mother, who must have known (they shared everything) but, as with the letter from Luis's mother, chose to keep it to herself. Even my Aunt Beatrice, who lived into my twenties – in other words, when I would have been old enough for her to talk with, to be recognized as fully human and not just a child – kept the existence of these people to herself.

Dora, of course, I knew about. My father revered his mother in death so much that I wonder whether he revered her as much in life. Something tells me he did – not just from the way he insisted that my mother be treated, but the manner with which he treated all women. If there was one way in which he was modern, it was his innate respect for women.

I never saw him patronize the wives of his friends – and he had profound respect for Frieda Gutman, the wife of his best friend Peter.

When he hired my mother before they were married, he may not have intended it, but he was hiring an equal partner in his business. The last years, when he got sick and the business started failing and they moved everything – including a shelf for samples and an oversized Telex machine – into a room in our apartment, and ran the business facing each other from across a pair of large, beige desks, I could see that they were equals.

On paper, he was the president and she was the vice-president, but I could hear from their discussions and arguments that they were absolute equals, that he respected her intellect, her business acumen, and above all, her judgment of people.

If there was ever something for which she reproached him, it was his naiveté – his inherent trust in people. She said he always gave people the benefit of the doubt – once – and that this was his Achilles' Heel. It used to make me laugh – the idea that he was so naive – because he always struck me as cynical. But maybe everyone seems cynical when you're a naive little kid yourself.

None of that explained why they had never mentioned Lily and Theobald. And again, I have trouble remembering their names. Their names aren't the same as mine – Hirschkind isn't Hickins. Hickins is my father's invention, not just of a new name, but of a new identity, a new beginning. Perhaps that's why he didn't tell me about them, and why I can't remember the name: there is no such thing as a Hirschkind; only Hickins.

I turn away from the wall, and rejoin my children, my wife, and these gentle German men.

"We want to show you something else," Klaus says.

A few short blocks away is the town hall, a stately, ornate affair straight out of the City Hall catalogue, 19th-century edition.

"There is a permanent exhibit here too," Klaus explains.

Inside is refreshingly cool and dark. The entire first floor of the left wing of the building is dedicated to another memorial to the Jews of Wiesbaden. On one wall is an alphabetical list of all the deported.

It is one thing to know your family was killed in the Holocaust, but quite another to see their names on a list. Here it is: it's official.

Your grandmother was here, and from here she was taken. Sobibor. I roll the word around in my mouth. Like an inarticulate marble. Sobibor. Sobibor. Abhorrent word, naked word. Maybe that's why they lied to me; Auschwitz has a more regal sound to it, like guillotine instead of chopping block. Less foreboding. Sobibor.

Thurman and Laura walk around, taking turns pushing Max in his stroller. For this fragment of time, I am no longer a father or husband. I am a grieving child. And yet even now, I am at some remove. I wonder why Wiesbaden finds it necessary to have a second monument – one to commemorate and one to resuscitate?

One thing – it feels good to be inside, sheltered from the oppressive heat and humidity outside. Even without air conditioning, the building is cool and the light dim.

On another wall are Plexiglas cases with photographs of some of these Jews, accompanied by short biographies. It feels more intimate, and sadder; you feel that instead of trying to be comprehensive, this exhibit is trying to be representative of what these people were in their communities: teachers, musicians, architects; fathers and mothers.

I look for something more about Lily and Theo. What professions did they have? What ambitions. Why did they never have children? Questions I will never be able to answer.

I can't help feeling we're staring at a children's school project, or visiting a macabre art gallery. I look at the pieces at some remove, like abstract paintings at a state museum. Some of the works are moving, while others "don't quite work for me."

I grow angry, resentful at the presentation. Yet at the same time, my heart is filled with gratitude. I realize it's contradictory, and I look at Laura for help. She can't help me – she doesn't know what I'm grappling with.

Max starts fussing in his stroller, so Laura takes him outside.

"How are you feeling?" Thurman asks, his voice catching in his throat.

I look at Georg and Klaus, who are again standing at a respectful remove.

"Sad. Angry. Grateful."

Thurman nods. "I understand." Then he says, "Thank you."

"For what?"

"For sharing this with me. For bringing me on this trip, for writing to these guys."

I don't feel like I deserve thanks. I feel like I deserve some kind of reproof for my profound ignorance, my complete lack of understanding, and for the shame I feel for being Jewish, for being part of a victimized tribe, shame for wanting reparations, as if any money I could give my children would bring back the victims or in any way bring us back to even.

Rationally, I know that's not what reparations are about. But rationality has little to do with the maelstrom of emotions I'm feeling.

Georg and Klaus have more to show us. We climb into Klaus's green Toyota and he drives us up to the Neroberg district, a toney residential area that overlooks the city. Klaus parks near the platform for the funicular, built in the late 19th century, which connects Neroberg with the town center.

We walk a short distance under well-tended Linden trees, which have a sweet, distinctive aroma. My ankle is cranky from being cramped in the car. Max is chafing from the confinement, so we let him run through the narrow public park that separates northbound and southbound traffic.

Across from the park are a row of mansions, built close together but quite luxurious. "This is where your grandmother lived, also her sister Lily and the husband," Georg says, gesturing to a three-story townhouse.

Then he points to the ground, to the small bronze plaques. "They are called stumbling blocks – *Stolpersteine* in German. They were invented by a German artist named Gunter Demnig. Anyone can order them," he says. "I don't think he realized how many people would want to order them."

"Stumbling blocks? For stumbling blocks, they're easily overlooked."

"Your grandmother planned to move to Amsterdam. I believe she bought a house there," Klaus says. "Have you been there?"

"She bought a house? In Amsterdam?"

"Yes, you'll see in the archives later. There is a bill of sale. We will show you."

Georg clears this throat. "Many German Jews believed they could have refuge in Netherlands, that it was safe."

I'm trying and failing to understand a simple premise. A property in Amsterdam. My mind is like a needle stuck on a record that won't go any further. "A property in Amsterdam? No, I never heard of this."

Klaus and Georg exchange a look that seems to say, "Didn't this family talk about anything?"

"My father died while I was still young," I say, by way of excusing my ignorance. "I think he wanted to protect me from confusion or something."

I ask myself: Do we own property in Amsterdam? Is this something I can claim for the sake of my children?

We drive back to the town center and order lunch at the shaded outdoor terrace of a Wiesbaden café.

Max leads Thurman on a chase around the pedestrian mall while we wait for the sausages to arrive, dodging fountains plashing water on the plaza, peals of laughter and release of energy for both of them. I smile at the rare pleasure of watching my two sons play together, and Laura squeezes my hand.

Across the plaza, a couple is getting married and their families are gathered on the steps of the town hall. They are dark-skinned, probably Turkish, or maybe Syrian. I wonder if they feel as foreign here as I do. I think about the Syrians who drowned off the coast of Italy because they were refused asylum. I wonder how many people who refuse asylum to others are alive only because someone granted asylum to their parents or grandparents.

I get a text from my sister Bette: *Michael sweetie, my a/c died and it's 100 degrees in here. I spoke to this guy, Bill, who fixes them. He says it will cost $150. Can you send me the money (please?? I know it's a lot to ask.)*

Sure, of course. Plus, maybe I'm richer than I know. Maybe I own a house in Amsterdam. Won't those people be surprised to know I own their house!

———————————

Klaus and Georg are regulars at the Wiesbaden historical archives, and they've ordered ahead for a number of documents to be available. They're the kind of things you cannot take out of the building, but that we'll be free to look at and even photograph.

It won't be the kind of place to bring Max, but I hesitate to leave Laura alone with him – he's restless and is going to try her patience.

I lead Thurman away from the table and stand close to one of the splashing fountains on the plaza so we can't be overheard. "Why don't you go alone? I'll stay with Laura and Max," I say.

"Why? You have to come," Thurman says.

"I can't leave Max for so long," I say, stumbling awkwardly.

"Are you kidding me?" he growls, "You can't say that – least of all to me."

"What do you mean?"

"You left me behind *for years!*" he says. "You left me behind with a crazy woman who doesn't even want to be my mother. Don't talk to me – ever – about not leaving Max behind for a few minutes!"

Whenever I argue with Thurman, the stakes are almost unbearably high for me. We see each other so rarely, the physical distance is so great, that it's difficult to not worry about a permanent estrangement from him. Especially given our family's history.

"No," I say carefully and softly. "That's not what I meant. I mean I can't leave Laura alone with Max for so long. He's being very difficult, you can see that."

Thurman shakes his head. I can see he has registered the new information, but he's still angry.

"You've come all this way. She can deal with Max for a couple of hours."

I look at Laura, sweating, uncomfortable, doing her best to smile, in a strange city, surrounded by foreign tongues, with a tempestuous three-year-old raging inchoately as he fights off waves of inexplicable and unexplained emotions crashing down around him.

But she's not crying. She's not my mother. Perhaps I've underestimated her.

We are not, as I would have imagined, alone at the Wiesbaden archives. History students from various walks of life need to further their studies, to find information, the kind you can only get at municipal archives. Not everything is digitized.

We are in a post-war building, natural light filling the lobby and hallways while the reading rooms are in the close-walled basement to prevent the sun's rays from damaging the artifacts. Some say that sunlight is the best disinfectant, but it is sometimes too harsh for the fragile details of history, the fragments of history we preserve so we can understand ourselves more fully. History can be like the smell of our beloved after a restless night, or like the putrid smell of lobster shells in the kitchen trash.

Georg and Klaus are greeted warmly by a young archivist with wireless glasses and short, curly blond hair. He hands them a pile of accordion files from the stacks. Inside are a number of yellowed documents and ledgers, some worn at the edges. Thurman and I sit across from each other at a large, light brown lacquered library table. Klaus sits at my side, across from Georg. It feels as if they have been sitting at this table, in this position, for many years.

Georg pulls an accounting book from one of the folders, which details my grandmother Dora's finances, while Klaus picks out my Aunt Beatrice's divorce decree from February 10, 1939.

Klaus drags his finger along the writing, haltingly translating the divorce agreement for me as he goes; Georg does the same for Thurman with the book of accounts. I hope the divorce decree tells me something about how my family lost the silk factory, or reveals something about the nature of my aunt's relationship with her husband – who may or may not have had more children.

"This says the motive of the divorce is Beatrice wants to emigrate to England and Reinhardt does not," Klaus says.

"The reason for the divorce is that she wanted to move to London? That's it?" I ask.

"This is what it says," Klaus says.

"Nothing about the Nuremberg Laws, or that she's Jewish and he isn't?"

"Nothing."

"In the US, you can divorce for irreconcilable differences – people have differences that cannot be fixed," I explain to the befuddled-looking Klaus.

"I'm afraid it doesn't say anything like that. It says Beatrice renounces her rights to the factory and the house and any restitution. Then they enumerate the pieces she is allowed to take with her."

Klaus turns the page and mutters as he gathers in his mind the pieces of English needed to continue. "Reinhardt must pay for the expense of shipping and the way for Beatrice to London."

"Her passage?"

"Yes, her passage." Klaus smiles at me. He points to a list. "These are the things she can take, it says one lipstick, three towels, two toothbrushes, one nail file, a bottle of nail polish, a bedsheet" he says, and pauses to see the effect on me. "There was also books, at first these were crossed out here – then put back on the list of things she could take back. And musical records."

The magnitude of the decree dawns on me slowly, as I begin to understand why Klaus picked this one to show me first. It is the official documentation of the destitution of a woman's life and property, the humiliating enumeration of her intimate personal effects.

I feel Klaus studying me closely. This is what life suddenly became for the flower of the German bourgeoisie during the 1930s.

This document is the fulcrum, it is the pivot point for my family's fortunes. For some reason that isn't clear, my aunt has given it all up – for the price of a steamship ticket. Generations of hard work, a legacy to the future, exchanged for nothing.

Klaus continues transliterating for me. "Reinhardt served in the

Freikorps," he says, pointing to a bit of biographical information about Dr. Lutz, the former dentist.

The failed dentist who marries a wealthy Jewish woman and dispossesses her of her assets at the first opportunity.

"What's the *Freikorps*?"

Klaus shakes his head, as at the folly of prior romanticists of phantom glories. "After the end of what they called the Great War, some officers continued fighting, supposedly on behalf of Germany in the east, but they were mainly attacking leftists. They assassinated Walter Rathenau, the German minister of foreign dealings. They stole and killed a lot of people."

"This is the man my aunt married?"

I think of Beatrice in the middle-class Jackson Heights apartment building where she lived for over 30 years. Her upright piano, the massive oak furniture, her discomfort whenever I cavorted on her sofa as a little kid, her fastidiously painted nails, her hair forever preserved by aerosol spray in an early-60s bob, her long, veiny legs perceived through loose-fitting nylon stockings.

I think of her devotion to classical music, of going to see The Beatles at Carnegie Hall because that was the thing to do in 1964; of her dating a Mr. Siegel for a few years, but never remarrying. Of her close relationship with my half-brother Walter, even after he and our father grew apart, accepting him for who he was even when our father wouldn't.

She never spoke about the bombing raids over London, just as she never spoke of her mother or father, her aunt and uncle, nor of their childhood in Germany. She never spoke of her former husband, nor the factory she left in his hands.

I think of this fussy woman with contradictory behaviors, her English affectation, the secretarial job she kept for more than 20 years and of her long subway commute to work, of seeing her gradually become smaller, angrier, more lonely, letting her nail polish get chipped, and then of finding liquor bottles hidden under her bed, of seeing her escorted by our building super back to her apartment after a naked dash through the apartment building, of finding slips of paper on her bedside table with notations: 2:15 and 10 seconds; 2:15 and 20 seconds; 2:15 and 30 seconds; 2:15 and 40 seconds; 2:15 and 50 seconds.

What was time to a woman who once lost everything she could lose and yet still live – her mother, her home, her business, her husband?

Across the table from me, Georg slams his hand on the varnished table, just as my father once did.

I look up, startled as a kid.

"This is impossible that people behaved so," he says.

Thurman passes me the document that drove the otherwise courtly Georg to such anger.

"Ach! It's the record of how they took your grandmother's money, bit by bit," Georg says. This is what he had meant to show me.

I scan the numbers as Klaus reads them off. The first entry is for 500,000 Reichsmarks. Klaus stumbles over his technical translation – not that I blame him; the language of legalized extortion is unfamiliar in any language. Taxes on Jews, on Jewishness, taxes for the upkeep of Jews, taxes for the transport of Jews, the murder of Jews. One thing is clear: the numbers keep diminishing, like a life's horizon, down to zero.

There is a notation next to the final number – Klaus explains the note means she was charged a tax for leaving the country. They deported her for being Jewish, and then fined her estate for the cost of her own deportation.

I lean back in my chair. These numbers are more tangible to me than an unseen property in the Netherlands, or even a factory that changed hands some 70 years ago. Here is a litany of the German government's theft of my family's assets. Surely there is still time to recover this. Yet I find the prospect exhausting. Do I want to spend the time that's left me in places like this one, under artificial light, among people who speak a language I don't understand, and whose history is one of bloodshed against my tribe?

"It's incredible," Klaus says. "We have done so much research and so much reading about your family, and now to meet you in person, the grandson of this poor woman." His voice catches. "Excuse me," he says. "I'm tired."

"I'm curious," Thurman asks Georg. "Was half-a-million Reichsmarks a lot of money?"

He snorts. "It's more money than I've ever had in my life."

In the back of the book of accounts is a notation from 1938, when Dora sells off her stock portfolio for 10,000 Reichsmarks. Ironically, she owns shares in companies like Hess and AG Farber, which contributed to the Nazi program. She pays half of her capital gains to the Mayor of Ansbach. I point to the entry and cock my head questioningly.

"More legal theft," Georg says. "She had to pay, like all Jews, 50 percent of all sales to the government."

"They left a very precise record of everything," Thurman says.

"Everything had to be legal," Klaus says. "There were laws about how to rob from the Jews, and everyone wanted to show they followed the law and took the money according to the law, not just highway robbery." He snorts derisively.

Around us are students and a few older people, all digging into some aspect of the past. I wonder how many of them are delving into the most sordid aspect of their history. I wonder how many of them feel shame, as Georg and Klaus seem to.

Klaus shows me the bill of sale indicating that Dora bought property in Amsterdam. I scribble the index number for the deed in my notebook.

"These are just some documents, some swearings – what is the word?" Klaus says.

Georg shrugs, then offers, "Vows?" He points to a telegram, from my father, from Yonkers, NY, dated November 3, 1947.

"Affidavits?" I suggest.

"Yes, affidavits, affidavits stating that Reinhardt is the trustee of the business. This is after the war. Here is an affidavit from your father."

"They must have been very close friends," Klaus says.

"Why do you say that?" I ask, incredulous.

"Your father makes him the trustee. He must have trusted him greatly."

It is impossible for me to convey how little that word would have meant to my father at that point: trustee. It was a terse telegram relating succinctly how little he cared for the world that had been destroyed in Ansbach, how far behind him he had put it all. Here, take it, do whatever you like, it's all the same to me.

I have learned from strangers in under 24 hours more about my family than anyone ever cared to tell me in a lifetime. My mother had to have known these things too, but she never shared them with me.

That my father just wanted to put it all behind him doesn't begin to explain or answer what happened to my heritage and that of my children.

My daughter Clara said recently that my parents behaved as if the future would never exist.

My father called me to his bedside one evening, a few weeks before he died. "I know you won't remember a lot of what I'm about to tell you. But try. Try to remember. It's important – you're going to be the man of the house," he said.

Ironically, I don't remember a word of what he said next, not a word. All I remember is repeating to myself the words, remember, remember, remember.

Maybe he told me where he hid the key to the secret treasure room hidden under the Kupfer silk factory. Maybe he told me where he'd put the deed to the house in Amsterdam that my grandmother bought but never had a chance to live in. Maybe he told me the secret to eternal life. I have no idea.

I do remember thinking, *Is he going to die, finally?* I imagined I would be free of the tyranny of his beliefs and his hierarchy of proper behaviors. And when he died, I felt remorseless. I felt relief.

But I have never been free of him.

What we find in the archives are acknowledgments that my father and his family existed, but nothing else. Acknowledgment, but no restitution, no compensation, nor even a sign of regret – let alone an apology.

It's not that my father, his mother, my Aunt Lily, and Uncle Theo never existed, but that their existence didn't matter. Losers, or worse — they were objects of pathos.

"Please," says Klaus. "A few questions."

When and where my aunt and my father died. Had I heard of such and such a relative? Why didn't my father file for restitution with the state? He takes notes of whatever answers I can give. I'm mostly reduced to shrugging and saying, "I'm sorry, I don't know."

"There were things I thought I knew or more-or-less knew, that I realize were false," I say.

Georg and Klaus have something else to show us. It is a stockyard on the other side of town, by the train tracks where the Jews of Wiesbaden were corralled and forced to walk up wooden planks like livestock into the cattle cars that were to take them to Auschwitz.

We drive to the eastern part of the city, past a commercial exhibition center, to an area about a quarter of a mile from the passenger side of the station. Black and red railroad cars idle on sidings. The road we're driving on is pocked with white gravel and littered with scraps of Styrofoam cups. The area is baked by the sun and mirthless. Looming in the distance is a disaffected slaughterhouse that serves as a memorial, a mural painted over the bricks on the front of the building.

Klaus drives towards the parking lot, only to find that it's blocked off by a handful of fat, muscular bald men wearing black leather jackets, tattoos, leather pants, and boots. Many of the jackets have lettering across the back – "Black Devils MC Germany." The insignia of the Black Devils seems to be a cross between a German eagle and a bat holding a pair of pistons.

"Nein! Nein! Nein!" one of the men shout at Klaus, stepping in front of the car and violently waving his arm.

In the back seat, Thurman and I exchange looks of incredulity.

"What is this shit?" Georg mutters from the passenger seat.

Klaus lowers his window, smiling benevolently, and says hello to the man waving us down.

"It's closed," the man says. "There's a concert here tonight."

Klaus nods, turns the car around, and finds a place up the road where he can safely leave it. We walk back to the parking lot, sweating under the late afternoon sun. No one bothers us as we walk in, but no one approaches us either – we're clearly outsiders, and not here for the concert.

Leather-clad men and women – mostly middle-aged – are wandering around, wearing the colors of different motorcycle clubs – the Wolfmen South-West, the Eagles, and of course the Black Devils.

A rock band is playing heavy metal on a portable stage – a warm-up band for the warm-up band.

Chesty blonde women sell Wulle lager and Bundaberg bitter beer from small kiosks. Hard alcohol and snacks are on offer at others.

We buy some bottled water and look around us, our heads hammered by the heat. I drink the water, which feels like it steams right out of my body.

The path to the memorial Klaus wants to show us is blocked off by waist-high barricades of orange plastic mesh.

"It's a shame we cannot go to the memorial," Klaus says. "I suppose the barricades are to protect the memorial from the members of the motorcycle club."

We peer at the memorial from some hundred yards, across a plain of sleeping bags and port-a-potties. Like history itself, the broad contours are easy to divine, but the details escape us. The mural is a reproduction of a photograph of some elderly people being helped into a cattle car, a testament to what happened, an attempted rebuttal to the doubters. From our vantage point, we can see that the people are old and frail. But who were they? Was one of them Dora Hirschkind née Kupfer?

———

Klaus drops us off near the memorial in the middle of town. Georg shakes our hands warmly, shrugs a small backpack onto his shoulder, and walks to the bus stop. Klaus hugs us, and gets back in his car.

"Are you thirsty?" I ask Thurman.

"Oh yes," he says.

We sit at a café and order a pitcher of house lemonade. The sun is going down but the temperature is still high.

"What do you think of them?" he asks.

"Klaus and Georg? Wow, great guys. You have to wonder, though. Why are they doing this?"

"It's maybe redemption time," Thurman says.

"I don't know," I say. "I'm trying to pull it all together. So many things I didn't know about our family."

"The house in Amsterdam?"

"Yes," I say, laughing at the absurdity of my ignorance. These are things everyone should know – that you think everyone does know about their own families.

I realize it's getting late. Laura will be waiting, and probably hungry. I feel the pressure of conflicting emotions: fatigue and anger; freedom and responsibility.

I'm grateful that we're sitting in the shade. I'm grateful for umbrellas and comfortable chairs, and for pitchers of lemonade glistening with condensation. I'm sure I'm not the first person to remark on the disparity between this scene and the one we've just witnessed from afar.

"It was easier being angry in Ansbach," I say. "In Ansbach, I felt like 'you people are living off the blood of my family.' Here, I'm more like, 'thank you for acknowledging that they existed.'"

"Thank you, but you still sent them to the gas chambers," Thurman says, smiling. It's not bitterness, exactly.

Max has taken to jabbing his finger in the air when he's angry at someone. After dinner, we sit in the hotel's private garden. Max has a temper tantrum and throws himself on the ground. Laura is exasperated. Thurman is trying to be the stern older brother, but I don't want him playing that role. They don't see each other often enough – I don't want Max to think of Thurman as an angry, scowling disciplinarian.

I'm tired and want to reflect on what we've seen, but Max keeps pulling me into the present. Perhaps it's just as well – perhaps the past has to be seen in the context of the here-and-now, the political and the personal. There are things happening today that encourage us to look away, to turn away from witnessing, but that history forces us to reckon with.

"Max, we're going to go up to the room if you don't stop," Laura warns him.

She looks at me, blowing a strand of undisciplined strawberry blonde hair that was tickling her nose. She is at the end of her rope with him, she wants me to take the reins, but I don't want to go upstairs just yet. The stars are still beckoning, the night sky and a glass of Scotch, Thurman roving in the garden as if looking for a tunnel back to some other time. Nothing can be settled in one night, but much remains to be said.

Suddenly angry, I get up from my chair and take three long strides to where Max is thrashing on the ground. I jerk him to his feet and swing him onto my hips. "Listen," I hiss furiously. "We've had enough, your mother and I."

I feel the fury rising in me, the fury that curses in all-capital letters. His own rage hasn't abated either. He squints his eyes and scrunches up his nose and jabs his little index finger in my face. I lean forward and bite it. Hard – just hard enough for it to startle him.

It wasn't premeditated. I didn't bite his finger off, but I growled. Abashed, I look at Laura and at Thurman for their reaction, and I can see that both of them are caught between shock and hilarity. They look at each other and place their hands over their faces. It looks to me like they're concealing peals of laughter.

Max is dumbfounded. "Daddy, why did you do that?" he asks, his voice quavering and close to tears.

"I told you not to point your finger like that," I say. "That's what happens."

"That's what happens?"

"That's what happens."

<hr />

Laura is asleep and I don't want to wake her, so I take the folders and go downstairs to the hotel lobby, which is empty save the night watchman staring at the flickering images on the 24-hour news channel. He turns the volume down when he sees me coming and walks back behind the reception desk, to the little office where he watches the closed circuit cameras showing nothing but a dark courtyard and a silent street.

I put the folders down on the big round marble table in the middle of the reception area, and I spread them out like a deck of cards with most of the face cards missing.

But the very act of putting them on a table is new, the perspective is new. I'm not in my dimly lit basement, shuffling yellowed papers in the dark.

I open one of the folders, the tab marked 1941 in faded pencil, and find a small photograph of a French highway sign. There's no comment on the back, no context that I know of. The sign reads Meillon. Come to find, it's a small town in France I'd never heard of before this moment.

In the same folder is another picture, a black-and-white photograph of three men – a priest, a man in military garb, and a man wearing a blue, white, and red sash across his chest, which is what mayors wear in France when they're on official business. "A mayor, a general and a priest step into a courtyard." It sounds like the beginning of a joke, only none of them are smiling.

They're standing in the courtyard of a single-story building, between the back of the main house and what look to be stables in the background. The military man, with his long, curved nose and short chin, is staring away from the photographer and towards the stables, while the priest is glaring sideways at the military man, and the mayor is staring balefully at the photographer. I hold it in my hands for a few minutes, wondering if I'm supposed to recognize any of these people. I flip the card over – it is signed, "To Max Hirschkind, from your friend Paul Mirat."

Max Hirschkind – that would be my father. But my father is neither of those men – and I realize he must be the photographer. Naturally, my father never mentioned either Meillon nor Paul Mirat either. Never mentioned, yet clearly important.

I take my phone out of my pocket and Google the name "Paul Mirat."

I read there was a Paul Mirat who was a painter, with works listed on a number of auction sites. What is he doing wearing the mayor's sash? As a painter, he doesn't even merit a Wikipedia entry. I Google Meillon. A village of 600 inhabitants near the Pyrenees. Wikipedia helpfully provides a list of all the mayors the town has had since the 1790s. It turns out Paul Mirat the painter was also Paul Mirat the mayor, from 1937 to 1945.

I stare at the photograph, peer into Mirat's face, the deep creases of his cheeks, his strangely luminescent eyes. Who the fuck are you? There's no one left to ask. Why was a photograph of the highway sign worth holding onto for all these years? Why has no one mentioned it before? If Paul Mirat was my father's friend, why had I never heard of him? The elder Mirat only died in 1967.

I knew my father had been in France during part of World War II, in a concentration camp in a town called St. Cyprien, near the Spanish border. Another Google map search shows that Meillon is very close to St. Cyprien. I knew he had helped that Mr. White/Weiss get a visa, although I never knew exactly how. Something to do with being a polyglot.

I dip back into the 1941 folder and carefully extract a yellowed postcard addressed to my father, care of Paul Mirat. It's from Peter Gutman, who I knew in my childhood as a skinny old man in a book-filled Washington Heights apartment, smiling always and always with a funny story about a childhood memory in the company of my father. I relished those stories, but they also saddened me, and on the drive back to our house in Queens, my mother would turn around from the front seat of our white Buick sedan and ask, "What's wrong, little one?"

I never knew how to answer because I wasn't sure myself.

"Nothing," I would respond, trying to prevent my voice from trembling. The last thing I wanted was for them to decide that Peter Gutman was another one of those bad influences, such as my brothers and sisters, from whom they needed to shelter me.

What made me sad was that even as a little boy, I knew I would never become as close to my father as Peter was.

Now I wonder why Gutman sent my father a postcard addressed care of this Mirat character. I hold it carefully, careful not to crease the aging card stock.

In his careful black ink handwriting, Gutman asks after Hilde – my father's first wife – and little Walter. *Is the boy over his tuberculosis?*

I pull another document out, this one a small, square government form, printed on very thin, wartime-issue paper. It declares that Max Hirschkind is employed as an interpreter and "making himself very useful" while living at Paul Mirat's house. Clearly, he's not living in the concentration camp at St. Cyprien.

It looks to me like Paul Mirat was doing something pretty extraordinary, hosting a refugee – a Jew no less – in his home. I look at the photograph of the three men again, at Paul Mirat's stare, and start to see something more – like a kinship born of shared despair.

Where are Hilde and Walter?

The folder yields more: a business card for Max Hirschkind, chief of sales for the Kupfer silk factory. A photo of a group of friends standing in front of the ornate Hotel Zirkel, their body language confident, cigarettes held jauntily, not realizing that the future was about to snap over their necks like a wolf trap.

Another find, another letter on wartime-ration scrap paper, addressed to my father at the French concentration camp at St. Cyprien. It's from his friend Fred Strauss. As I read it, I am overwhelmed by the audacity – and the irony of it. I remember Strauss from the few parties my parents hosted at our house, as one of the rich, portly, self-assured people my parents tolerated like they tolerated all their friends.

Reading this letter, I realize how long my father must have known

Strauss, and cannot imagine the exact proportion of camaraderie to contempt in which they must have held him.

To Mr. Max Hirschkind

Ilot I Section III Baraque 16
   Camp de St. Cyprien
   Cyprien–les–Perpignan
   Pyrénées Orientales, France

August 24, 1940

My Dear Max,
   I just received your registered letter and I am very pleased indeed to hear that you are in good health even if you are in a prisoners' camp over there. Furthermore I am only too pleased to hear that you have finally located your wife and your boy even if they are in another camp. I trust the camps are not too far apart?
   With regard to the financial matter I sent your request for assistance to my (I hope still wife) Lisl and I have asked her to deal with it. I am very sorry (and totally unhappy and downhearted) to have to inform you that Lisl left our home about 2-1/2 months ago, more or less when I was away on a long business trip. She has joined the harem of Mr. Wolf, my former partner. She was convinced by this family, and was very nicely treated, so that she made up her mind to leave me and our home, and as far as I was informed, she is living in the same house as Mr. Wolf, where also Mrs. Mailaender lives. Mrs. Mailaender got a kick, and for the time being, she has served also. There are some other women such as Mrs. Eisman who is one of candidates, and many others. The only reason Lisl has given me for leaving is that she had to work too much, namely in the home in the morning and in the office in the afternoon. Besides that, a phony accusation that I am a pessimist. Both reasons are phony and without any foundation and can be laid ad acta *without any discussion. The reproaches I make myself are that I had a lot of confidence in my wife and as she was always ridiculing the way of Mr.*

Wolf and his family, I did not dream that something like this would turn out.

It dawns on me, reading this letter more than 70 years after it was written, that Mr. Wolf is the man I knew as Uncle Fred, whom my parents called the Gnome (behind his back, of course). They mocked his habit of buying a new car every three years. They mocked his materialism and his avarice, and they exchanged innuendo about his lasciviousness that was only partly lost on me. He was short, of course, with liver spots on his bald pate. This smiling Buddha of a man, with a good-natured twinkle in his eye, was the lothario described in this letter by Fred Strauss.

I realize now – and only now – that Lisl was my half-brother Walter's aunt, the sister of his mother Hilde, who died mysteriously in Cuba.

Like Fred, Lisl was also tiny, and by the time I knew her, with gnarled fingers tipped with garish red nail polish, as hard to imagine as the prize over whom these men struggled as it is impossible to see Fred as a gentleman suitor.

The worst thing is that Mr. Wolf induced Lisl, who in my feeling is not under her free will, and who is more or less a bundle of nerves, to empty during my very long absence the whole vault of the money of our relations.

You can believe me, Max, my troubles are big, and as I feel personally obliged to you, I wrote you everything in full.

I now come to your request for financial aid. As Lisl has taken away all my money, including those that we saved together, and I strictly refuse to go against her, as she is still my wife, I wrote to her and asked her to comply with your wishes.

I have also been in touch with your uncle Paul Kupfer, who has opened an office on Union Square in Manhattan.

So you can see, my dear Max, although you thought you are the most unfortunate and unhappy family, you are more happy than I am here in New York.

I am purposely not including any money because Lisl will no doubt send it to you and I am in very narrow straits. With very best regards and sincere wishes, to you, Hildegard and Walter, I remain, very sincerely yours, Fred.

PS I hope you can feel how I am alone, alone without ANYBODY!! I want to be together with you – alone I shall perish and die!

Of course, we could never invite both couples to the same party, but I got the idea that my parents vastly preferred the company of the Strausses to that of the Wolfs.

But Wolf was family – in a way I didn't understand then – while Strauss... now that I've seen the letter, I fail to understand why my father tolerated him at all. Imagine being in a concentration camp, days away from being sent to Auschwitz along with 5,500 of your fellow Jews, and getting a letter from a whiny friend saying not only is he worse off because his wife left him for his business partner, but that he can't send you a lousy ten bucks.

But then I imagine my father finding excuses for him: he couldn't know what was going on over there, no one really knew for sure, and we all know how hard it is for a man when he's been betrayed by his wife.

That held serious weight for my father.

Shortly after being liberated from the concentration camp, arriving in Cuba, and establishing himself and his family with the rest of the "international community" in Havana – meaning Jews, intellectuals, leftists, and free-thinkers from all over Europe, but not black people, Asians, or immigrants who hadn't come from families of means – Max walked in on his wife Hildegard in the arms of her old paramour – her flame from the days before she met my father.

According to my mother, there were things my father could never forgive. He was slow to anger, but once he got there, it was as implacable as Menelaus's hatred of Paris.

My father told Hildegard, the woman with whom he had shared a child, a war, and a persecution, that "they would stay together for the sake of the boy, but would never again be as man and wife."

In other words, no more fucking. He was exiling her to a lifetime of conjugal loneliness. Three months later, this woman who hated the water and never went swimming was found dead in the ocean. My mother says the presumption was suicide, and that my father prevailed upon the coroner to rule her death an accidental drowning so that Walter wouldn't have to live with the knowledge that his mother took her own life.

I find another letter addressed to Paul Mirat, this one from the Prefect – the administrator of the local region. In very formal bureaucratic language, the Prefect rejects Mirat's request to allow Hilde and Walter to also stay at his house – they have to return to Gurs.

Gurs, I also learn from Mr. Google, is the location of another French concentration camp also located just outside Meillon, and which I had also never heard of before.

I carefully lift another yellowed, cigarette-paper-thin sheet out of the folder.

It's a typewritten poem – at the bottom, two dashes, and the words Max Hirschkind. My father – a man who not only didn't write poetry, but didn't even read it because all he cared about was facts – had written a poem. I am baffled. Hadn't he told me on more than one occasion, "Everything that can be said has already been written?"

The poem is in German – I cannot read it, except for the title, which is *Was Ist Meillon?*

Even I know what that means. "What is Meillon?" And I wonder, what indeed is Meillon.

Are the poem and photographs from Meillon something more than signposts from a past no one bothered telling me about?

I realize that I miss my father. I have argued with him all my life. About who has or hasn't prostituted themselves; about hope (he was anti and I was pro); about masturbation (ditto), about the inexhaustible and ever-inventive human spirit.

I still want to prove to a man more than 40 years dead that, despite whatever doubts he may have had about my character, I lived up to the purpose he had sired me for – to take care of my mother in her old age.

Now, however, I also want to ply him with questions no one else may be able to answer for me, and that I didn't even know were questions until after everyone who could answer them was dead. Who was Paul Mirat? *Was Ist Meillon*?

Had they forgotten about it? Thought I wouldn't be interested? Was the omission deliberate, and if so, why?

I Google Paul Mirat again. I scroll past the links to the auction sites, past the ad for a genealogy and DNA test site. I see an article in the *Sud Ouest* newspaper from two years ago.

The article described a retrospective of Mirat's work the city of Pau held at town hall; his grandson – also named Paul Mirat – was a town official quoted in the article. There is no mention of the War or refugees or Jews, nothing about stables or generals or priests. Nothing but the paintings.

I find the town's official website, and write to the "contact us," hoping they will forward my message to Paul Mirat (the grandson, obviously). The gist of my message is this: your grandfather seems to have sheltered my father at his home. I know my father was also imprisoned at the concentration camp at St. Cyprien. The rest is a mystery to me. I'd love to talk to you."

In the morning, I share my discoveries with Laura and Thurman over breakfast in the hotel's very formal drawing room.

"Remember all those times she told you, 'don't forget to look in the box. The key is in the middle drawer of my desk'? She wanted you to find this," Laura says.

"Why didn't she just tell me about this while she was alive? Why didn't my father tell me?"

Laura shrugs. "People back then didn't talk about the war."

"I guess," I say. But I feel there's more to it than that. "Thurman, how good is your German?" I know he studied German in school.

I carefully hand him the poem, which he takes only after having wiped his hands on a thick white napkin. He shakes his head. "I can't read this, but I know someone who can." He takes a picture of it and hands it back to me. While I place it back in the folder, Thurman emails it so someone who studied German or is dating a German or something to that effect.

I check my own phone. There's the usual slew of news alerts – and amazingly, already a response from Paul Mirat. "What a welcome event to receive your email this morning," he begins. "People sometimes stop to leave flowers on his tomb, strangers I never knew, but to have someone like yourself communicating with me – what joy!"

"Look, it's him," I say, sharing my phone with Laura and Thurman.

Laura looks down at her own phone.

"He's the former head of communications for the town of Pau. He wrote a book about Pau during the Gilded Era; also a book about Pau as a center of aviation, and he's written a book about the cultural links between Pau and Newport, Rhode Island," she says, reading from her phone.

I can't resist – I call him. He speaks a delightful English, an English born in the 1960s and honed by years spent as a wine merchant in London, escaping the weight his name carries in Pau and Meillon. "No one knew who I was, it was delightful!" he says.

"You must come to visit," he says.

Pau is further south in France than I've ever been. It's a four-hour train ride even on the rapid TGV.

The south of France, free France, although it was hardly free at all, is where my father's life paused as if perched on a wire, the fates debating if this was the end of the line. Auschwitz or Ausland, Birkenau or the Berkshires, Sobibor or SoHo.

My mother was in the South of France too, at around the same time. Sitting in a swank hotel in Wiesbaden with two sons and a wife, is it that farfetched to imagine my mother and father could have crossed paths in France? And then recognized each other 15 years later in a small office in the Hotel Breslin in New York City, where my mother applied for a job opening? I imagine this dialog:

"You seem familiar..."

"Were you ever in the South of France? An enchanted spot just north of the Spanish border?"

"Why, yes! A delightful place of barbed wire and machine gun nests."

"So you know the spot!"

Everyone who has parents knows this feeling – that our mothers and fathers communicate on a wavelength audible only to dogs and to each other. That they have known each other since the days of Noah, since the days in Babel when everyone still spoke the same tongue, that they have secret secrets that give them superpowers.

I wonder then: did they *actually* meet in the South of France?

Paul Mirat's grandson is still alive, my only living link to the past – and to any answers I could possibly get.

10

'WAS IST MEILLON'

Our train chugs into Pau. It's a smaller station than you'd expect for a city with an administrative center, but it's modern, with glass walls that let the ample sunshine in, and small kiosks selling snacks and beverages. We are in a different setting than Paris or Germany or Prague – the sky seems a darker shade of blue, and the mountains hug the skyline. White villas dot the hillside.

There is, however, no sign of Paul Mirat. After a few minutes of standing around and pacing nervously, I pull out my phone and scroll through our email exchanges. There doesn't seem to be a disconnect – no indication that I've communicated the wrong day or time.

So where is this gregarious retiree?

"Is that him over there?" I suggest.

Thurman looks at the picture Paul sent me so we could recognize him. "Looks nothing like him. Our friend Paul is in his sixties, he doesn't have any hair on his head, he has big ears and a big nose. This other guy—nothing like that," Thurman says.

Eventually, Paul pulls up in a sporty blue sedan. He hops out lithely and walks briskly towards me, as if he'd known me all my life. I put my hand out to shake, but he instead embraces me in a powerful hug.

"So happy to see you, dearest," he says. He gives Thurman the same enthusiastic welcome. "This is all the bags you have? Of course, you're not staying very long. I wish you were staying longer. Let's get out of here!"

It's just Thurman and me – a long train ride followed by a monotonous conversation is too much to put a little kid through, so Laura agreed to hang back with Max in Paris.

We get into Paul's car, he puts it in gear, and peels out of the railroad station drop-off area like a teenager on Sunset Strip. And he hasn't stopped talking.

"You're lucky, or maybe you're unlucky. The Tour de France is here tomorrow morning. You can see it if you want, although I don't know why you would."

"Yes, you mentioned that in your email. Like I said, we're not really interested."

"Good. But you never know with Americans – so crazy about sport, no?" He slams on the brakes and yells out the window at a large bearded man standing in the middle of the street with a tape measure and a clipboard.

"Hey, George, what the hell are you doing? Shouldn't you be at work?"

"Ah, Paul," the guy responds. "We can't all live the life of leisure like you can!"

"Ha, ha," Paul shouts as he puts the car back in gear and roars through the narrow, winding, ancient streets of Pau.

High above us looms the castle where the Protestant King Henri IV of France was born.

Paul drives us along the magnificent boulevard des Pyrénées, which overlooks a valley and a miles-long panoramic view of the Pyrenees mountains.

He stops again and yells at another friend, a woman working with a film crew.

"I'll see you later," he says. Then to me and Thurman, "We're invited to a party this evening. Of course you'll come."

"You know a lot of people," I say.

"Roots," he says. "My family has been here for 20 generations – that we know of!"

"Twenty?"

"Yes, and of course I worked for the city, so you know, I met a lot of people."

Gradually, the city falls away and Paul rockets down a two-lane highway bordered by small farms, shrubs, and thin stands of trees. The Pyrenees loom everywhere.

I see the road sign before I can read it. It's a relatively small sign on the side of the road, a marker with red lettering. Meillon.

Paul pulls into the courtyard of his house – the one his family has lived in for hundreds of years, dozens of generations, innumerable wars. He seats us at a long oak kitchen table, with a bowl of fruit and half a baguette from the morning still wrapped in thin, waxy paper.

He walks around to the other side of the table. "I hope you're hungry, kids. I'm going to make us some lunch," he says.

He starts cutting the stems off mushrooms that turn the stainless steel sink black with dirt, then throws the mushrooms into a pan with a couple of large pork cutlets.

"Can we help?" Thurman says.

"No, I love doing this. Ever since I retired last year, this is my simple joy. I make lunch for myself and then I smoke a bowl of *la locale* and relax, then I make dinner for Pascale so when she gets home, all she has to do is put her feet under the table."

He grabs a handful of small, red tomatoes that he washes and cuts.

"*La locale?*" Thurman asks.

Paul giggles. "It's not bad. Whenever one of us goes over the hill to Spain – Spain is right over there you know, halfway up that mountain road there, whenever someone goes up there for cigarettes, we ask around, anyone need cigarettes. It's rude not to ask. It's like four euros a pack instead of 15 or whatever they make us pay over here. Help yourself. And along the way, you pick up some of *la locale* if you're of that ilk!"

He pulls a pack of cigarettes out of his denim shirt pocket and tosses it casually on the table. It's almost enough to make me want to start smoking again, just the casual gesture of friendship, of bonhomie.

"One of my friends grows it up there – we call it *la locale*. It's not bad, just good enough to get you in the mood for a nice nap. No one ever beat up their wife because they had too much of it," he says.

I look around and try to drink in the space. I realize I won't be here for long, and that I'll want to remember it. Klaus Kalbkopf didn't let me upstairs where my father lived while growing up, but here I am in the house where my father lived instead of dying.

The sink is to the left of the stove where Paul is frying up the pork chops; to the right of the sink is counter space for prepping food; the counter runs the length of the room, and on the floor there's a wooden crate filled with local peaches. The room looks like it could have been painted by Paul Cézanne.

The front windows and open door give us a view of the generous front yard where Paul parked his car. The back and side windows look out on a garden and stables.

"Those peaches in the crate there – we're having them for dessert," Paul says. "They're *roussanne*, you can only find them here in the Bearn region. Legend has it, Henri IV once said his only regret upon taking the throne in Paris wasn't converting to Catholicism, it was not having *roussanne* peaches to eat."

"I guess they don't travel well," I say.

Paul shakes his head. "You can't find them anywhere but here," he says proudly, while dicing up tomatoes.

"Paris was worth a mass, and also *roussanne*," Thurman says.

Paul laughs. "I'm sorry I didn't ask – no one is allergic to anything? You never know these days," he says.

"I'm Jewish – I don't eat pork," I say.

Paul's face caves in, he instinctively backs away from the frying pan with the sizzling pork chops – he's crestfallen, embarrassed, he can't believe he hadn't thought of that before.

"Kidding – I'm totally pulling your leg," I say.

He laughs uproariously. "You Americans, you never know," he says.

"You're right," I say. "Those people are crazy."

"My dad is an exception to the rule," Thurman says.

"I've never known a people so obsessed with religion and so lacking in morals!" Paul says.

"Really?" Thurman says. That rubs even the anti-American in him the wrong way.

"Look, they're wonderful people individually. Your father for instance – a darling!"

"And you've only scratched the surface," I say.

He puts his hand on the kitchen counter that separates us. "I could tell from your first email to me, I could tell this was a man with a beautiful heart."

You should tell my wife, I think.

"Did you know?" he says. "The world's first school for aviation was established here in Pau by Orville and Wilbur Wright?"

He jogs around the kitchen counter to the bookshelf on the far wall and pulls out a book that he hands me. "It's a little monograph I put together when I was heading communications for the city of Pau. It's a little better than a tourist brochure, don't you think?"

I flip through the book, pictures of the Wrights – including their sister, a tall woman who apparently played a much bigger role in their lives than she's given credit for in the history books. She could be my aunt, a woman much admired for her mind, and very much alone.

"All the rich Americans came to Pau, did you know that? It was the high-society set from Newport, Rhode Island. They made it just like their home. All the big fancy villas – those are the rich Americans from Newport, Rhode Island." He repeats the name-place like a shibboleth.

I gaze idly at the paintings on the wall. "Are those by?"

"My grandfather? Some of them. Others are by his brother, Yves." He points to a painting of a sad looking boy with big brown eyes, seated in a wooden chair, his face in his hands, gazing into a frightening future. "That one is the Spanish refugee. My cousin says he remembers the time right after the war that this old Spanish lady came into the house she looked at the painting and said, 'that's my Roberto!' and she started to cry."

Thurman gets up to take a closer look. "Dad, this reminds me of what was his name, Juan Antonio, your mother's first husband?"

"Yes, he and his family were refugees from the Spanish Civil War," I explain for Paul's sake.

"We were used to helping refugees, from 1936. That was what Gurs and St. Cyprien were built for, but they were built as temporary camps, with wooden planks between cabins, roofs made of tar paper, that kind of thing. They weren't designed to be torture camps either, but it was torture living there.

"When they told my grandfather they didn't want him to fight in this war because he was too old, but to prepare for the refugees they knew would be coming – from everywhere, they warned him, and they were right – he took one look at the camps and said 'no, not on my watch.'

"People started coming from Belgium – early in the war, they were called traitors for capitulating so fast, until it was our turn to capitulate! – and then the low countries you call them?"

"Yes," I say. "The Netherlands."

"Yes, the Netherlands. And the east and the north of France you understand, our own countrymen, my grandfather wouldn't conceive of making them live in camps. My grandfather also had huge sympathy for the Spanish, and the Jews.

"Okay kids," Paul says. "Let's eat. Enough with the fun and games – we have serious work to do after lunch."

I meet Thurman's gaze.

"Hospitality must be in your gene pool," Thurman says, reading my mind.

"This is really incredible," I say. Tears start welling up in my eyes.

"Come on, come on, let's eat," Paul insists.

Naturally, the pork chops are tender and tasty and the mushrooms delicious. The tomatoes have nothing in common with

American tomatoes, the taste and texture of which have been bleached and blended out of existence by industrial farming.

Then the peaches, the *roussannes*. I might as well never eat another peach.

Suddenly, I'm sobbing. Here in this room where my father survived, dreaming perhaps about a meal such as this, perhaps even eating one as tasty if not sparser, here in this room where the world that is disappearing for my children is still recognizable, although the warning signs of our great extinction are as audible as proclamations of the Final Solution; here in this room, a moment of ephemeral beauty is given to me, given me to share with my son Thurman, this moment of love freely given, of Paul Mirat the elder in spirit and Paul Mirat the younger in the flesh, and the bright sky and the stables through the window and the Spanish boy and the workshop of freedom and revolution, of Max the gaunt refugee with his gaunt wife and their stubbling child, the sickly tubercular Walter who lived through all this only to die of AIDS, and the exploding sunlight in the absolute calm of the afternoon, the stillness of the postprandial pause, the expert thumbing of a cigarette rolled with loose tobacco mixed with *la locale*, of dishes cleared, throats cleared, a pat on the shoulder, a squeeze of the arm, I'm coming back to the present knowing it is suffused with the past.

Paul Mirat.

The grandson of Paul Mirat leaves the table and walks into an adjoining, book-lined room. He pulls a book off one of the shelves, a thick book that resembles a book of accounts, comes back through the French doors, and hands it to me.

It's a register of names in a leather-bound ledger, sheets of accounting paper with green lines, an accounting of hundreds of names, their places of birth, the dates of their arrival, the linens they were given, the linens they returned, the dates of their departure. As if he were an innkeeper with the instincts of a certified public accountant.

"He did this right under their noses," Paul says. "He didn't falsify one thing, he didn't hide anything. It was all right here in this register. But – he never showed the register to anyone. He forgot, I guess."

A sly grin crosses his face.

"He forgot to show it to anyone. He just kept it here – it was here all the time. If anyone had wanted to look. You know, he convinced the entire village, there were 600 people, no one told the Gestapo, there were 600 people in this village – and they hid over 2,000 refugees. Two thousand, can you imagine?"

The pages are stiff and yellowed, each name separated from the next by a thick black horizontal line drawn with a ruler. Each name written in the same cursive handwriting. Most of the names have ID photos next to them.

My father was so skinny. I have never seen a picture of him as a young man before. I've seen a few of him as a boy, and have many of him taken during my lifetime. But this – a man in the fullness of his adulthood, but robbed of the fullness of his power, his blue eyes paler than I remember through a pair of glasses that blur his irises imperceptibly, the look of a man with the weight of the world on his shoulders.

His wife Hilde – the first time I have seen a picture of her at any age. She has been blotted out of our family's memory like an ink stain rubbed out by a crumpled tissue, like the history of Ansbach and the Kupfer silk factory. She is scowling through sunken eyes, angry at the world for having tricked her into thinking everything would be all right.

There is no photograph of sickly Walter, just his name.

And then more names, pages and pages of names. I flip the pages idly, as if looking for an old friend in my high school yearbook.

Quick math: 220 pages, nine names per page, that's 1,980 names, 1,980 human beings. Stuffed into a village of 600 people.

I look at Thurman. "And Donald Trump says America is full," I say.

"Your Donald Trump," Paul says. "Proves what I say about Americans loving religion so much."

He hands me a spliff. "Let's go outside," he says.

We walk into the garden where a small fountain stands in the center of the rough grass. "That was already there when your father was here," he says. "He saw this fountain. He looked at it."

Now it's my time to look at it. Only I want to look at it through the eyes of Max as he was then, to feel what he must have been feeling, but I can only look at it through the eyes of the Max that I knew – the angry, embittered, unforgiving Max, the Old Testament Max I was brought up with.

I never knew the Max of Meillon, the Max capable of writing a poem, of loving an ugly woman, the Max who carried his family on a journey across Germany, Belgium, and Cuba. Who brought the remnants of his family to New York. I don't know the Max capable of such courage.

In Meillon, he wore specs. In New York, it was thick bifocals. Something changed, obviously. It isn't hard to understand why. It's harder to understand why not – those people who didn't change, who remained optimistic and happy, like my father's childhood friend Peter Gutman.

Or like old Paul Mirat, the mayor. As far as I can tell, he was ever the same, before, during and after the war. Like France itself, eternal and self-knowing.

We cross the garden to the stables, weather-worn, wooden planks a-shamble, shards of the afternoon sun casting fragments of sunlight through a shadowland of the past. A stack of metal cots are lying against a wall. Paul points to them.

"That's what many of them slept on," he says. "Metal cots, a few pairs of sheets, a few small bedside tables, a few chairs, much of it for common use – it was a hardship for those people, many of them used to having servants, big houses, sometimes even running water inside their homes.

"Some of them slept here. Some of them in the house. My grandfather and his wife rented another house in the village so they could make room for the refugees."

––––––––

Paul takes us on a short walk through town. There's a stone cross two stories high at the roundabout at the one main intersection, and from there we walk past the elementary school. We walk along a narrow lane called rue de la Judée – street of Judea – and Paul stops to talk to an old woman watering flowers in her front yard, wearing a blue kerchief and red rubber wading boots.

"Madame, how are you?"

"Paul, good."

"These are my friends from New York," he says.

"I'm not really from New York," Thurman says.

"Ah, I see," says the old woman, ignoring Thurman's aside. She is soon joined by her husband, a small, thin old man with a pencil mustache, a blue cap, and a yellow *Gaulloise* cigarette between his lips.

"We went to New York last year," he says. "It was a lot bigger than here!"

The five of us laugh at the absurdity of the comparison. I'm surprised this couple has wandered outside the boundaries of their own province, much less to the United States. I've known people who lived 45 minutes away who had never been to New York City.

"What brings you to Meillon from New York?" the man asks.

"This man," I say, pointing to Paul. "This man and his grandfather."

"Mrs. and Mr. Petibon were little kids during the war," Paul says.

"Kids, well, I'd say a little more than kids," Mr. Petibon says.

"Yes, well, you were here when all the refugees were here."

He points to me. "His father was one of the refugees my grandfather hid in the house," Paul says.

"Ah," Mr. Petibon says, nodding.

"If it weren't for him, I wouldn't be here at all. Not in Meillon, not anywhere. Nor him," I say, pointing to Thurman.

"Ah," Mr. Petibon says. "That's good. That's very good."

As if I had told him it was going to be sunny for the rest of the week.

"How long are you staying?" Mrs. Petibon asks.

"We're going back to Paris tomorrow," Thurman says.

"Ah, very good," she replies.

"Very good," Mr. Petibon says.

We stand smiling stupidly at each other for a few seconds.

"We never talk about those days," Paul says.

"No, we haven't talked about it," Mr. Petibon agrees.

"Why is that?" Paul asks.

Mr. Petibon shrugs. "I suppose there's no point, it's the past," he says.

"Weren't you afraid?" Paul asks. "I mean, what you did was dangerous. Everyone in the town knew what was going on, a lot of people were hiding refugees. Weren't you afraid?"

Mr. Petibon looks at his wife, takes the cigarette out of his mouth and looks at it, as if wondering where it came from. "Sure, we were all afraid. It was a frightening time," he says.

"We were just saying how lucky we've been," I say. "Our generation. We haven't had to endure war or penury."

Mr. Petibon nods, unsure of what to say next.

"Well," says Paul, "have a good afternoon."

"Yes, see you later," Mr. Petibon says.

"I have a couple of boysenberry pies in the oven," says Mrs. Petibon. "Why don't you take one later?"

"Okay, maybe I will, but don't wait for me," Paul says. "We're going to a party later."

We walk on a few yards and Paul pulls on my shirt. "You see that? They're still afraid! It's as if they're afraid of the past in retrospect."

———

He leads us to the newly christened Paul Mirat cultural center. There is a large photograph of his grandfather affixed to the outside wall. The former mayor looks like a cross between FDR and Jean Gabin, the old mid-20th-century French movie star, with a strong chin, a cigarette holder clamped between his teeth, and a steely-eyed determination on his face.

"His eyes," says Thurman. "They're brilliant."

The current mayor of Meillon, Patrick Buron, meets us in front of the cultural center – I recognize him from the newspaper article I saw when I first Googled Paul Mirat. He jokes about who has the keys. Paul has the keys, of course. I get the sense that Buron may be the current occupant, but that the office belongs to the Mirats in perpetuity.

Inside is a retrospective of Paul Mirat's life, his early years in London, his military career, a picture of him with US soldiers in Maryland, and reproductions of his paintings – mainly colorful caricatures of local notables in chaotic street scenes.

The exhibit also includes a blow-up of a letter from a group of Belgian refugees thanking Paul and the entire town. Thurman, sensing the emotion rising in me, touches my shoulder as I read.

To the Mayor of Meillon

Dear Mr. Mirat,

You see gathered in your midst these men, these women, these children, those who are designated using the painful name – "the refugees."

Abandoning their homes and their most cherished belongings, fleeing their countries or departments before a cruel horde, they have wandered where luck would take them, across this beautiful and afflicted France, from city to city, from town to town, in search of a single night's bed or a few days' temporary shelter.

What providential luck, what happy inspiration guided our steps towards Meillon? It matters little, for here we are, and here we stayed! We have learned to appreciate Meillon and its inhabitants, but especially we got to know Mr. Mirat!

It's you, dear Mr. Mirat, who comforted us, who had this gift of making yourself beloved by those who came to you, and who no longer think of themselves as poor refugees, but almost as your compatriots.

We will never be able to properly exalt to our families and friends the warm welcome that you gave us, and that we will never forget.

From the Belgian and French Refugees at Meillon, July 1940

The Belgian and French refugees, among whom most certainly was my father, and whose language, whose turns of phrase, whose way of mixing sentiment with formality, I feel I recognize in this letter.

My father never once mentioned, let alone exalted, this man and this place. I wonder whether he felt he could never do it justice, whether we – his family – would disappoint him by failing to be suitably impressed – or whether the subsequent events of this period would cause him to forget all the good, to banish it from his mind as surely as the Nazis banished in him the possibility of ever again setting foot on German soil.

"The refugees mention not just Mr. Mayor Paul Mirat, but the entire town. This is very important," Paul remarks to Buron. "This isn't just about my grandfather. This is the entire village. I don't want people to think this is just about one man," he says.

"No, quite right," Buron says. "It's important that people know that. They are all part of history."

"Brilliant PR move," I whisper to Thurman. "Put the focus on the village so people don't resent honoring his grandfather."

Thurman nods at me and smiles.

Someone knocks at the door.

"It must be Roger!" exclaims Paul.

It's indeed Roger Dupont, a stringer with the local paper. Another display of Paul's PR skills.

Dupont is lanky, with tufts of white hair curling out from under a floppy hat, He's wearing a green polo shirt, wireless specs, and has a small camera around his neck.

"Roger, this is Michael Hickins, the former *Wall Street Journal* editor-in-chief! Patrick of course you know."

We shake hands. His handshake is weak – not soft, but not energetic either. There's nothing about him that screams reporter.

"Not editor-in-chief – just an editor," I say.

"He's too modest!" Paul cries out with some exasperation.

"And this is my son Thurman."

Dupont nods at Thurman, who nods in return.

"How about we start with a photograph?" Paul says. "The sun is still high, it's perfect lighting."

"I don't have a lot of time," Roger says. "I have an important match coming up in a few minutes."

"Oh come on, your *pétanque* can wait!" Paul says, laughing.

"No, there are three other fellows, you know how it is," Roger says quite seriously.

We gather outside the Paul Mirat cultural center, and Roger poses us for the shot. "The Americans in the middle, please," he says.

"I'm not really American," Thurman says, but Roger ignores him.

We all squeeze into the frame and Roger snaps his picture.

"We can talk at the house," Paul suggests, and we follow him the five minutes it takes to return to the Mirat family home. Thurman finds himself walking next to Buron, who starts talking about his plans for a more environmentally sustainable village.

Back in Paul's dining room, I make a show of admiring his grandfather's celebrity portraits and the historical paintings of Henri IV, Gaston Febus, and other notables from the Bearn region. But I find Yves' paintings more significant; old Paul Mirat's brother was not only the better artist, but his subjects were more modern – his treatment of that Spanish boy with his chin in his hands and long bangs covering one eye was more meaningful and human than all the spectacles and all the grandees of Pau combined.

"So how did you find out about Meillon?" Roger asks me.

"I was looking through some of my mother's stuff – she died recently – and I came across a picture of the road sign for Meillon. It just spoke to me – why would my father have that picture. He wasn't very sentimental. And then I found this poem he wrote – a man who didn't write poetry or even care to read it."

"What was it about?"

"The title is '*Was Ist Meillon*' – what is Meillon. It's a good question. It's in German, so I haven't been able to read it yet."

"I see. And then you found Paul?"

"Well, there were also these photographs of Paul Mirat the mayor — Paul standing with a couple of village notables – autographed to my father."

"He was with Father Regnier and Colonel Ryback," Paul puts in. "My grandfather and father both told me about Father Regnier – he was mean to children. And Ryback – a hero of the Resistance, a former Czech spy."

Roger keeps scribbling notes. "What do you make of all this?" he asks me.

"I'm amazed and grateful, of course. And Paul has been such a wonderful host," I say.

"Yes, I see," Roger says.

"Roger, this is important," Paul says. "This isn't about me or just about my grandfather. He was perhaps a hero – but the townspeople went along, they were all complicit."

"These poor people of Meillon, you know what happened to them? They developed PTSD. They had been so afraid all those years, even though they went along, that they fired my grandfather in the middle of his last term. In 1944, his deputy came into his office and said, 'Paul, you have to go now. You're finished, the people don't want you as mayor anymore.'

"So he left the building and never went back. And even after the war, no one said anything to him at all."

"No one talked to him?" Roger asks.

"No, they shunned him. They had been so afraid for so long that they punished him, almost retroactively – they said, this is what you get for making us so afraid all those years. It wasn't until 1947, the prefect of Pau said this isn't right, and they gave him the *Légion d'Honneur*."

Roger asks me a few more questions about my impressions of Meillon and my reaction at seeing the spot where my father had been sheltered. Then he rises spryly from his chair.

"Well, I'm off to my *pétanque*," he says.

Thurman walks to where the mayor is sitting, seemingly transfixed by the stables visible through the window.

"We're buying a hydrogen-powered bus," Buron says. "We're trying to get farm credits for our local farmers to help them with the transition to organic farming."

Thurman nods, and segues into a discussion of honey bees. The mayor nods enthusiastically, and I wonder whether Thurman would move here to help in some quixotic attempt to create a utopian commune of sorts.

The mayor and the reporter take their leave, and Paul decrees that it is nap time. "We're going to a party tonight. I'm not like you young kids – I need my sleep!"

"Wait, I want to ask you one more thing," I say.

Paul walks up to me and smiles. "Anything at all, my dear friend," he says. I feel he would give me literally anything I needed.

"I was wondering if you have, if there's anything, I mean, something my father might have left behind. There's so much I don't know about him. I didn't have him for very long."

"Ah my dear friend, I'm afraid not," he says, squeezing my arm.

I nod quickly; I realize I am grasping at the most unlikely of straws.

Thurman and I sit alone in the living room.

"So what do you think?" I ask him.

"The world wasn't built to last," he says.

"What do you mean?"

"I mean, did you notice Roger didn't ask me a single question? I'm the future here. And this all concerned my grandfather. You'd think he'd have asked me at least one question!"

"He asked how to spell your name," I grin.

"Exactly."

He pauses. "You know, everyone has known about this climate emergency for decades. The first official warning about global warming was in 1979, the United Nations issued an alarm, and said the countries of the world have to do something. But nothing has been done. The world does not believe in the future, it only believes in the past and the present."

I am old enough to remember 1979. The year my hero Thurman Munson – my son's namesake – died in a plane crash. I don't remember any warning about global warming, though.

"Shall we follow Paul's example and take a nap?" I suggest.

"I'm not tired. You go ahead," he says. "I'm going to do some writing."

I go back outside through the back door to the garden where my father once gazed at the small fountain as he was on his way, perhaps, from the stables to the mayor's office for an earnest conversation, or perhaps to share a joke. I think about the can of my mother's ashes still with my knapsack by the front door, where my father probably loitered so he wouldn't have to return to his ugly first wife's side.

I wonder if I should scatter her ashes here, in the garden, and just be done with it. But why? What are the odds that she was anywhere near here? I would have to ask Paul for permission, and then he would have to ask his wife, and it would be a whole thing. I can't just dump some ashes on the ground. I decide this isn't the place – there's no connection to my mother here, so far as I know.

Later than evening, Paul's wife Pascale, Thurman and I get in the car with Paul, who drives as if he needed to light up the night with his rocket-propelled Peugeot. We quickly find ourselves in a small town called Nay, where a friend is having a dinner party for 20 guests, a last bash before everyone scatters for their vacation homes, their annual trips to Greece or Italy, cruises through Nordic fjords, or long flights to Australia.

Paul introduces me to everyone individually. Everyone seems interested in meeting the American, no one seems particularly surprised, and no one seems particularly interested in why I'm here. It's a conversation starter for sure, but tell me about what it's like to live in New York. Is it true white people can't walk safely in Harlem?

Thurman is the only guest under 50, but fortunately, the hostess's 23-year-old daughter Sylvie is there as an indentured servant. As soon as possible, she breaks out of the kitchen and starts chatting with Thurman while they share a cigarette in the garden.

Sylvie is slender, with a softly rounded face, long hair and doe-like brown eyes. She looks at Thurman as if he were an alien god who has just hopped off his intergalactic transport vessel. She isn't sure if he's going to ask her to join him on a journey of a thousand light years, or whether she'd even want to go. Change is scary, especially for the young.

There is something safe about being French, as is made apparent by the group of 20 people squeezed around a dinner table. The suitably bearded college professor, the portly real estate agent and his hot, poufy-haired real estate agent wife, the thin-lipped woman of means with a classic string of pearls around her neck, the bald gentleman who made his fortune in lima bean imports, the tweedy world traveler and his predictably unsatisfying tales, each of them trying without trying to impress one another, to remind one another of why they're worthy of friendship. They are comfortable allowing their Frenchness – the culture which circumscribes their opinions and their values – to define them.

This one is the acknowledged expert in new medical advances, this other one knows more about Nouvelle Vague cinema and its influence on the younger generation of cinematographers than anyone else at the table.

By unspoken assent, no one talks shop, except as the subject of gentle teasing.

The professor is allowed to complain about the poor quality of student the school system is producing these days. But that's about it.

"They care more about protecting bees than our historic monuments," the real estate agent complains.

"Who cares about monuments if there's no food to eat," says the guy who's all about scientific discoveries.

"What's the point of being alive if we can't remember history?"

"Guys," says the hot wife. "Those two positions aren't mutually exclusive!"

Every once in a while, someone steps outside to have a smoke and to "see how the young'uns are doing."

The young'uns, Thurman and Sylvie, are standing very close to one another, their lips almost caressing as they talk. She's back to school in Paris in the fall. She doesn't see herself living in a big city, though, and neither does he. He rather likes Meillon.

There are differences of opinion, of course, and perhaps rivalries under the surface of certain relationships, but everyone in the room shares in a complacency more inherited than earned. They are French above all things, steeped in a culture built slowly over many hundreds of years. No one believes anything will change that first principle – not even the tides of history.

Trump, a dangerous populist demagogue, can be elected President of the United States, but that's our problem. That can't happen in France. Never mind that three (2002, 2017, and 2022) of the last five presidential elections in France have featured a National Front candidate advancing to the second round – that doesn't seem to shake their confidence in the essential qualities of France. It can't happen here. I've heard that before, and I can only hope their confidence is deserved.

The party breaks up at around 11. People kiss on cheeks. Thurman and Sylvie exchange phone numbers.

Paul drives, fast and drunk, beating back Pascale's protestations that maybe she should drive.

I do not want to leave Max an orphan in this way, but I'm helpless to change anything.

We do get home without incident and stand together in the entryway of Paul Mirat's house. Our departure tomorrow will be too rushed by the early hour for a proper goodbye.

"What was your father like?" I ask Paul.

"He was old. Not the sort to play soccer with the children, you know?"

The town is dark, outside the window is dark, and I think about what it would have been like in the dark 70 years ago, dreading the Gestapo raid, the late-night summary execution as certain as the cock's crow. The very existence of Paul Mirat seems more and more like a miracle. Just like my own.

I pull the Paul Mirat in front of me into a long embrace. He smells like alcohol, tobacco, and a little bit of *la locale*. It's a smell I want to bottle, not because it reminds me of my father, but because one day it will.

The next day, on the train back to Paris, my mother's ashes still in the can of Swee-Touch-Nee Tea, I get a little carsick watching the specks of countryside speed by.

Thurman and I have stopped talking for the moment, each of us absorbed by the pocket-sized computers we're holding in our hands. Yes, technology makes it easier to communicate; I cannot think what my relationship with Thurman would be if we hadn't had the Internet to bring us together during the years we spent apart. But now we're both sucked into the rabbit holes of information that keep us on separate sides of the prison glass.

There's a story in the *Washington Post* that catches my eye. A museum in Germany has released a new batch of photographs from Sobibor, thanks to the generosity of the descendants of a concentration camp officer named Johann Niemann. Knowing now that my grandmother was killed in that camp, my attention is drawn to the details.

According to the Post article, Untersturmführer Johann Niemann was killed by his charges at Sobibor in October 1943. He "was lured to the tailor's barracks with the promise of a leather jacket and killed by an ax to the head."

I cheer silently, pumping a virtual fist. Here is the response to all those who claim the Jews died like sheep, without putting up a real fight.

The trove of photos, kept by his widow and then grandson, include over 300 pictures – him with his men, both in uniform and in civilian clothes, or of him in the prison yard where Jews were selected for work gangs or death. There is one of him posing on horseback in front of train tracks that thousands of Jews were forced to cross on their way to the gas chamber — a staging area for his hero shot.

Then it hits me – this Niemann is the man who killed my grandmother. The actual guy who pulled the switch that turned on the gas that choked the life out of her. The man who gave the signal. The man who picked the tattoo numbers to be gassed that day.

"What are you looking at?" Thurman says.

I can hardly get the words out. "They found some photographs of a Nazi concentration camp guard. The one who killed her. Killed Dora."

I show him my screen, and we huddle around my phone as I flick through the pictures. I stop to look at one photo, taken with two other men sitting on a stack of hay and bricks in front of a building where people were "euthanized."

The men he's pictured with look like you imagine killers look, with profound scowls, eyes that are sunken with the horror of what they do. But not Niemann. He has big, prominent ears, his shirtsleeves are rolled up — he could be a university student, a chemist, a postal worker. He could be a writer or someone who used to date your sister. But he isn't those things. He is the leader of men who commit murder on a mass scale. He's proud of himself, but in this picture at least, not inordinately so. He is quietly confident. He has the air of man who, while accomplishing much, relishes above all the company of his friends on a warm afternoon in the early fall, just a few hundred yards away from a building where people are being cremated. The air has a slightly tangy odor to it.

He is Niemann. He is the bloodiest killer of the three friends. It is he who personally supervised the killing of my grandmother, Dora Kupfer Hirschkind.

I realize it's a cliché to talk about the banality of this monumental murder, but it is jolting to see not just the image of the man who killed my grandmother and my cousins, but to see him in so many postures and affects: the man of action on horseback, the man surrounded by his friends, the man overseeing the organized, mechanized murder of thousands — including, again, my own grandmother.

The man was clearly enamored of his own rank, his spectacle, and his accomplishments. According to the Post, he was promoted in 1943 by Heinrich Himmler himself — the architect of the Final Solution.

Then, after his murder, he was honored and celebrated by the Reich, given a posthumous medal, his achievements read aloud for his wife to hear. He served the Fatherland by murdering tens of thousands of Jews, Romani people, gays, and suspected Socialists and

Socialist sympathizers. Along with my grandmother Dora, her sister Lily, and Lily's husband Theobald.

"I never heard of Lily and Theobald until last week," I say. "Now I have also learned their killer's name."

I realize I'm trembling. I am not sure what I'm feeling, but I suppose it is a mixture of anger and sadness. I have always been afraid of my own anger, and it occurs to me that perhaps my father was also afraid of his own murderous rage.

It occurs to me that maybe when I shout at Max or when I pound my fist on the dining room table, I'm really pounding out my father's fury at what happened to our family in Germany and in the killing yards of Poland.

I wonder if I know what I'm feeling, or if I just know what I'm supposed to be feeling. And what is Thurman feeling? Is he giving me a hug because he feels how (he thinks) I feel, or because he knows it's a way to express empathy – and one he doesn't actually feel?

Can his feelings be real if mine are not?

Can I know whether my feelings are real or just the byproduct of education, propaganda, and manipulation?

I try to look into Niemann's face, to see whether I can discern any feeling in it. I pinch out the photo on my iPhone, trying to perceive an expression of some kind, but there really isn't one. You would think that someone so evil would *look* evil, but if anything, evil is the washing out of expressiveness.

People tell me all the time that I look angry or sad or some certain way. I may not know what I'm feeling sometimes, but apparently those feelings are visible to others. Maybe this is what separates me from Niemann.

Niemann killed helpless people by the bulldozer-full. His ability to discard his humanity made him a hero of the Reich.

I won't say he could be me, because that would be to dishonor the dead. The dead did not die at the hands of a namby-pamby public relations man too squeamish to pick up a dead mouse in his own basement. A man who would cry at the death of a beloved athlete who died in a tragic plane crash, and want to name his son after that athlete.

No, they died at the hands of a man capable of slaughtering thousands, of breathing deeply the fine autumn air slightly tinged with the acrid scent of human remains, and of ensuring his white shirt is immaculate for the photograph.

Thurman squeezes me and buries his head in my shoulder blades. He breathes me in. I cringe, and I realize what I'm feeling is that I'm not worthy of his love.

11

WHAT IS MEILLON

They didn't know when she died. The date of death recorded on stumbling stones and on the memorials that have her name is May 8, 1945, but that's just a symbolic date – the date the camps were liberated. Despite all the meticulous record-keeping for which the Nazis are renowned, they don't know exactly when or how Dora died.

Maybe when her train arrived at Sobibor, they culled her from the larger group, along with other elderly and infirm, and ordered her to walk into the woods – to the infirmary, they were told – where she was summarily shot and dumped into a pit, pell-mell and limbs akimbo. Or maybe she was marched into camp and then eventually ordered into a cinderblock room into which they pumped carbon monoxide gas that killed her.

They didn't know. They couldn't tell my father when they killed his mother. They didn't bother with this kind of record-keeping.

The deep-seated fury he carried inside for the rest of his life wasn't because they killed her, I realize, but because they couldn't tell him when. Or how.

They recorded so much for posterity, and proudly. But not that. The ending of the life of some stupid Jewess was not worthy of recording.

I feel the fury rising in myself. And suddenly and for the first time, I recognize it. It's the same fury I feel when Max – my son – jabs his finger in my face, or when my wife says something that disappoints me. It's a fury that rises so quickly it doesn't have time to get red or black or any color – it's just a white flash, a flash-bang tympanum of rage.

It's a rage that stifles my breathing.

It's the rage that made his hair turn white at the age of 48.

It's a rage so violent I once broke a tooth clenching my own jaw.

Rage he kept like a memento of bygone years, passed down to the next generation, rage that felt all the more violent because it had no real target. How do you kill Nazism?

I had known two versions of my father. The reasonable, slightly rigid Max, heir and defender of traditional mores. And the trembling-with-fury Max who towered above me, glowering or slapping the shit out of me.

Maybe he never talked about any of this because to talk was to remember and to remember was to relive that Herculean rage that could not be sated. Not only Herculean in scope, but as destructive as if it had been driven by the Furies themselves.

Hercules slaughtered his wife and children while under the spell of the Furies who deranged his mind, while my father left behind a trail of death and abandonment: his first wife, Hilde, died in Cuba, ostensibly the victim of accidental drowning. My mother told me she probably killed herself because my father caught her having an affair with her former lover.

Did my father treat Walter with less-than-kindness because he suspected his son was really the child of his dead wife's lover?

That none of my mother's other children – my two sisters in particular – managed to remain under his roof into adulthood, but were either thrown out of the house or married off to their boyfriend – can that be attributed to my father's fury? Impossible to say for sure. But the furious zeal with which he protected my mother from the angry words of her children was not commensurate with what any reasonable person would consider proportional. And yet it was all in the name of protecting my mother from the cruelty of which he was unable to protect his mother.

A rage against the Nazis, yes, of course. But also this: he didn't do enough to save his mother. Perhaps if her sister and his uncle had immigrated to America, instead of going to Wiesbaden, she would have followed them there. Perhaps they could have left before it was too late, before the Nazis had figured out a way to keep them alive in Germany until all their money was gone, before killing them.

Perhaps this is why he never mentioned Lily and Theo – it was their fault his mother didn't leave! Perhaps they convinced her that Wiesbaden was a safe haven.

But at the end of the day, the only person he could blame – because he was the only survivor, along with Walter, who was a blameless child – was himself. He, Max Hirschkind, was at fault for failing to save his mother's life. He led his wife and child from Germany to the Netherlands and Belgium, and then from France to Cuba. He left his mother behind, his willful, stupid, gullible mother, who listened to her sister and her brother-in-law instead of listening to him.

He couldn't, wouldn't kill himself. It was a sin, first of all, and it was the act of a coward, and he couldn't do that to Walter even if Walter weren't his legitimate child. So he did the next best thing. He killed his name.

Sure, Hirschkind was hard for Americans to pronounce, and they would probably misspell it. So what else is new? What else is that he changed it before he ever set foot in the US, before anyone ever had a chance to mangle it.

He changed his name so he'd never have to hear himself associated with those people and that name, those stupid Hirschkinds, and he wouldn't have to think about the woman he left behind, his mother, every time he signed his name.

He never talked about the fury, but he passed it along to me. Not the narrative, which may have been as painful as it would have been liberating – but the rage, a rage that has so often caught me unawares, and which has often left those I most love bewildered and afraid.

He also never talked about it because, well, who was he to complain? We were the victors, the saviors of democracy and the civilized order, the vanquishers of evil, the bulwark against man's tyranny over man. Who were he and his sister Beate – victims, the lame of spirit, un-American in their passivity and pessimism – to dampen the mood with his recriminations, his demands for reparations, and his wounds?

We Americans won, we move on, we spend, we expend, we gash the landscape with our highways, and stain the skies and drain the waters, we waste heedlessly what is in abundance and are miserly with humility that is in short supply.

How can machines ever hope to pass the Turing test when humans can't reliably pass it either?

Thurman raps his knuckle on the door twice and comes into Philippe's bedroom.

"My friend translated your father's poem into French," he says. He shows it to me.

I feel as if someone has handed me a newly discovered fragment of Heraclitus.

It brings tears to my eyes before I even start reading – just the very idea that I'm reading words he maybe never intended for anyone to see. That he had buried, like everything else about the war and the Holocaust that he buried under a mountain of bad decisions, fury, thoughtlessness, and willful neglect.

Words from my long-dead father about a long-dead past that was being brought back to life. Finally, some last words from my father not tinged with irony or sarcasm.

WHAT IS MEILLON

What is Meillon?
> A quiet little speck
> near Pau
> in the department of Basses Pyrénées
> and yet when I look around...
> I realize there's something more.

What is Meillon?
> A miraculous life-raft
> Which saved us from the sea of excrement that is Gurs?
> That's a comforting thought!
> But what if this raft breaks apart?

What is Meillon?
> A slice of Eden,
> Where everyone does what he likes?
> No respite for hunger, but
> where talk of food takes the place of food?

What is Meillon?
> A mere mailing address
> That consumes reams of letter paper and airmail envelopes?
> A telegraph outpost that receives news from abroad
> Even if we ourselves are not here in spirit?

What is Meillon?
> A giant question mark?
> a period, full-stop, after imprisonment?
> A place to recover our strength?
> To fight against bureaucracy and madness,
> Lost letters and lost time?

What is Meillon?
> A springboard to uncertainty?

a shield from grim reality?
A nest of brave and furtive souls?

What is Meillon?
    This nest of farmlands
    Is fatefully linked to all of our lives
    And may have more to give us all
    than we can recognize today.

What Meillon is?
    The answer eventually becomes obvious; we'll nod as we sip our tea,
    "Yes, yes, Meillon, a quiet little speck
    Near Pau
    in the department of Basses Pyrénées."
    And nothing more.

– Meillon, 15.8.1941.

12

IS THAT A PARK?

"You win. You do realize that, don't you?" Laura says.

We're back in Yorktown Heights, in bed. Max is asleep in the next room. I'm about to strap my CPAP machine over my head – very sexy if you're into that kind of thing.

"I mean, you've outdone your father. In every way. You've made more children. You've done more with your life. More of your children are functional. Your wives and exes are all still alive," she says.

I laugh, not because it's funny. It's a laugh of relief.

There isn't going to be any money, at least I don't think so. It turns out that my father (and my mother) received a few hundred dollars a month in survivor benefits. I'm sure that helped my mother get through a few rough months.

Compensation claims for survivors and their heirs from what became West Germany expired more than 45 years ago, and those from East Germany expired in 2017 – two years before I heard from Luis for the first time, or learned of the current/continued existence of the factory.

We've stayed in touch with Klaus and Georg, and they in turn connected me with Dr. Ekkehard Heubschmann, another German archivist who specializes – incredibly – on the Ansbach archives. Dr.

Heubschmann uncovered yet another way in which the Nazis despoiled my family – forcing them to buy property that turned out to be a place in the Theresiendstadt gallows. For this, they had to shell out around 81,000 Reichsmarks – the equivalent of $650,000, adjusted for inflation.

As for the property in Amsterdam, the records have been lost, ironically because the Allies firebombed the office of the notary in Cologne where they were kept.

I make it a point to text or call Luis once in a while; he still lives in Hawaii, and I look forward to visiting him there – someday.

Camille texts from time to time.

I've also reconnected with George Gutman, the son of my father's best friend/cousin Peter Gutman. He too was unaware that our fathers were related.

He told me that in 1960, a year before I was born, he and his family visited Ansbach, and my father's factory in particular. He remembers that when they got to the reception desk and asked to see Frau Lutz, who was expecting them, the receptionist corrected them: she was Frau Doktor Lutz; the honorific is so prized by the Germans that it attaches even to their spouses.

I wonder if a man married to a woman with a PhD is also allowed to call himself Doktor.

George was too young when this visit occurred to have been aware of the reason for their visit, and I have to wonder myself: was Peter asking for something on my father's behalf, a memento he may have left behind? Were they simply catching up on old times?

Again, it's something I'll never know.

I wrote Renate Lutz a letter, and had it translated into German, asking her if she knew anything about the family saga, or any details about the transaction that left the factory to her father. She never replied.

I can easily live without the financial reparations I was half-hoping for. It's hard to get too wound up over something I didn't expect for the first 55 or so years of my life. Would it be nice to have something to pass along to my kids? Of course.

More deeply unsatisfying is the lack of answers to so many

questions that I realize were always in the back of my mind, but which I never expressed. There are stories you never question, no matter how unlikely they are, because you heard them as a child, when you processed everything without questioning. Received wisdom you store in the part of your brain labeled "incontrovertible facts."

"You think he would be proud of me?"

Laura reaches across our king-sized bed and puts a hand on my arm. "Yes, yes I do," she says.

And then she kisses me. She slides her hand behind my head and her nails bite into my scalp, and her leg swings over and across me. "Ah," she says. "Ah. Ah."

We decide to attend our Reform congregation's Yom Kippur services. I haven't attended services at all since my father died.

Rabbi Robbie explains the meaning of each prayer before we begin reciting them because we're a Reform congregation, and the assumption is a lot of the congregants are like me and don't attend services very often.

Apparently, I have been thinking about this holiday all wrong. All along I thought it was the day God decides whether or not to punish you; silly me. It's not for nothing that it's called the Day of Atonement.

To atone. It's up to me to make reparations, also.

"The Talmud explains that we can ask forgiveness of God and that is a personal matter between God and each one of us, but that is the easy part. The harder part is seeking forgiveness of people we have wronged, and forgiving others for the wrongs they have done us. And we must also strive to forgive ourselves, to give ourselves a bit of a break, because we're all human, we're all doing our best, and it isn't always easy. We don't always live up to the best of ourselves, and we need to be able to forgive ourselves," he says.

A sob escapes my chest at the word forgive.

Laura, sitting in the chair next to mine, puts a delicate hand on my arm.

I hope no one else notices my crying. It seems absurd.

I'm crying for those Jewish relatives I'll never know, and for my father whose faith was taken from him, and for my mother whose fear of admitting to herself that she betrayed her older children was always just below the surface of her bluster, and for my siblings who died in neglect and shame, and for my own shame and self-doubt and for my little Max because of the horrid world we're bequeathing him.

I remember my last Yom Kippur ceremony — when my father was still alive, but barely, and in agony, and the other old men of the congregation implored him, "sit, sit," when we were supposed to stand for this or that portion of the service.

He would obey the other old men, wincing in compliance, furious with his body, furious with his god, furious with me for all our weaknesses.

"This is the moment we can forgive others and ourselves," says Rabbi Robbie.

I'm still not sure how formally, or how often, I want to make religion a part of my life. But I know that I don't want the Nazis to have taken this away too. Perhaps my father had lost his faith well before the rise of Hitler; perhaps he lost it when he lost his mother, and he cursed the god who allowed it to happen.

Of all the goods my family could have handed me and my children, this might have been the most precious: the connection we share to each other through our shared rites and beliefs. The community that is created and the bond that exists between us, and is strengthened by our adherence to a particular faith.

I'm not talking about the afterlife or salvation or walking with God. God may have never existed, or existed a long time ago and died, or retired to a beach in far Andromeda Galaxy (they say the sunsets are spectacular). What I'm talking about is a recognition of the quiet that connects us and maybe all things, and the gentleness of recognition of that quiet.

I'm talking about a small, quiet voice that spoke to the prophet Isaiah and that is the source of life, the source of life's spirit, and that is the source of strength and life's ongoing desire to keep living.

I don't know what I call that today, but it's that ongoing desire to keep living that allowed my father to make it all the way through, wounded and mutilated, and to express his modicum of hope for the future by procreating me.

And here I am, trying to overcome those scars, and to pass along that spirit to my children – particularly the youngest of them, Max.

A few days later, a little after Halloween, Laura and I go out for dinner with her parents in Kingston, the Upstate New York town that is trying to become Brooklyn North. We have Max with us, and he gets a little restless between the main course and dessert, so I take him on a walk around the neighborhood.

"Is that a park?" he asks after we've gone a few feet.

"No, that's a parking lot," I say.

"Is that a park?" he asks when we've gone another few feet.

"No, that's another parking lot."

He's quiet and we walk hand in hand. I love feeling his little hand in mine; it's the best feeling in the world; better than sex.

"Is that a park?" he asks as we cross the street.

"No, that's a graveyard," I say. I immediately regret my choice of words. Why couldn't I have just said churchyard? The public relations man in me is appalled.

"What's a graveyard?" he asks.

"It's where we plant people when they're dead," I say. Again, I want to stuff the words back in my mouth, but it's too late.

"We plant them?"

"Yes, when people die, we put them in boxes and then we plant them in the ground."

It just gets worse and worse.

We stop at the wrought-iron fence and peer into the darkened graveyard. Tombs from the Revolutionary War era loom gray and undecipherable to the naked eye. He stares quietly for a while.

"Is Dolly dead?" he asks about our deceased, geriatric cat, who died about a year ago.

"Yes, she's dead," I say.

I'm helpless now, trapped in a brutal reality of my own wording.

"I miss Dolly. Can we see her again?"

"No, she's dead. She's gone."

"Is she in a graveyard?"

"Yes."

"Did we plant her in a box?"

"No, we only plant people in boxes. Well, some pets too I guess. Some people plant their pets in a box, but it's dumb."

"Why is it dumb?"

"Because. They're gone."

"What happens when they're gone?"

"Nothing. They're just gone."

"Can we see them again?"

"No, they're dead, and when you're dead, you're gone.

"That's why it's important to be careful when you cross the street," I add, desperate to get something positive out of this conversation, something Laura won't absolutely kill me over.

"What does dead mean?"

"It means you're not alive anymore," I say. "You're gone. No more life."

"Why can't you just go to the life store?" he asks.

I am struck dumb. "There's no such thing as the life store," I say finally.

"Yes there is," he says. "I saw it a long, long time ago, when I was a little baby."

"Mommy's probably worried about us by now," I say. "We should go back."

When we get back to the restaurant, Max runs over to our table.

"Mommy," he announces in his best teacherly voice. "When people are dead we plant them in the ground!"

Laura looks at me and mouths "What the fuck?"

I shrug, palms upward.

She shakes her head at me.

When we get home, I steal a glance the can of *Swee-Touch-Ne Tea*, which still holds my mother's ashes.

"What am I going to do with you now?" I ask.

It occurs to me that I have a lot of work to do. I want to help Paul Mirat win broader recognition for Meillon, and for the world to remember the name of Paul Mirat.

What is Meillon, one may ask. It is a speck of a town in the south of France, crowded up against the Pyrenees, where you eat well and have some laughs, and no one talks about the heroism of their ancestors.

ABOUT THE AUTHOR

Michael Hickins is the author of the acclaimed short story collection *The Actual Adventures of Michael Missing* (Alfred A. Knopf), the novels *Blomqvist* and *The What Do You Know Contest*, and the memoir *I Lived in France and So Can You* (Dzanc Books).

Hickins was born in Queens, New York, and plied his trade as a journalist with *The Wall Street Journal, eWeek,* and *Women's Wear Daily*. He lives with his wife and son in the deep dark woods of Westchester County, New York, USA.

AMSTERDAM PUBLISHERS HOLOCAUST LIBRARY

The series **Holocaust Survivor Memoirs World War II** consists of the following autobiographies of survivors:

Outcry. Holocaust Memoirs, by Manny Steinberg

Hank Brodt Holocaust Memoirs. A Candle and a Promise, by Deborah Donnelly

The Dead Years. Holocaust Memoirs, by Joseph Schupack

Rescued from the Ashes. The Diary of Leokadia Schmidt, Survivor of the Warsaw Ghetto, by Leokadia Schmidt

My Lvov. Holocaust Memoir of a twelve-year-old Girl, by Janina Hescheles

Remembering Ravensbrück. From Holocaust to Healing, by Natalie Hess

Wolf. A Story of Hate, by Zeev Scheinwald with Ella Scheinwald

Save my Children. An Astonishing Tale of Survival and its Unlikely Hero, by Leon Kleiner with Edwin Stepp

Holocaust Memoirs of a Bergen-Belsen Survivor & Classmate of Anne Frank, by Nanette Blitz Konig

Defiant German - Defiant Jew. A Holocaust Memoir from inside the Third Reich, by Walter Leopold with Les Leopold

In a Land of Forest and Darkness. The Holocaust Story of two Jewish Partisans, by Sara Lustigman Omelinski

Holocaust Memories. Annihilation and Survival in Slovakia, by Paul Davidovits

From Auschwitz with Love. The Inspiring Memoir of Two Sisters' Survival, Devotion and Triumph Told by Manci Grunberger Beran & Ruth Grunberger Mermelstein, by Daniel Seymour

Remetz. Resistance Fighter and Survivor of the Warsaw Ghetto, by Jan Yohay Remetz

My March Through Hell. A Young Girl's Terrifying Journey to Survival, by Halina Kleiner with Edwin Stepp

Roman's Journey, by Roman Halter

Memoirs by Elmar Rivosh, Sculptor (1906-1967). Riga Ghetto and Beyond, by Elmar Rivosh

―――――

The series **Holocaust Survivor True Stories WWII** consists of the following biographies:

Among the Reeds. The true story of how a family survived the Holocaust, by Tammy Bottner

A Holocaust Memoir of Love & Resilience. Mama's Survival from Lithuania to America, by Ettie Zilber

Living among the Dead. My Grandmother's Holocaust Survival Story of Love and Strength, by Adena Bernstein Astrowsky

Heart Songs. A Holocaust Memoir, by Barbara Gilford

Shoes of the Shoah. The Tomorrow of Yesterday, by Dorothy Pierce

Hidden in Berlin. A Holocaust Memoir, by Evelyn Joseph Grossman

Separated Together. The Incredible True WWII Story of Soulmates Stranded an Ocean Apart, by Kenneth P. Price, Ph.D.

The Man Across the River. The incredible story of one man's will to survive the Holocaust, by Zvi Wiesenfeld

If Anyone Calls, Tell Them I Died. A Memoir, by Emanuel (Manu) Rosen

The House on Thrömerstrasse. A Story of Rebirth and Renewal in the Wake of the Holocaust, by Ron Vincent

Dancing with my Father. His hidden past. Her quest for truth. How Nazi Vienna shaped a family's identity, by Jo Sorochinsky

The Story Keeper. Weaving the Threads of Time and Memory - A Memoir, by Fred Feldman

Krisia's Silence. The Girl who was not on Schindler's List, by Ronny Hein

Defying Death on the Danube. A Holocaust Survival Story, by Debbie J. Callahan with Henry Stern

A Doorway to Heroism. A decorated German-Jewish Soldier who became an American Hero, by Rabbi W. Jack Romberg

The Shoemaker's Son. The Life of a Holocaust Resister, by Laura Beth Bakst

The Redhead of Auschwitz. A True Story, by Nechama Birnbaum

Land of Many Bridges. My Father's Story, by Bela Ruth Samuel Tenenholtz

Creating Beauty from the Abyss. The Amazing Story of Sam Herciger, Auschwitz Survivor and Artist, by Lesley Ann Richardson

On Sunny Days We Sang. A Holocaust Story of Survival and Resilience, by Jeannette Grunhaus de Gelman

Painful Joy. A Holocaust Family Memoir, by Max J. Friedman

I Give You My Heart. A True Story of Courage and Survival, by Wendy Holden

In the Time of Madmen, by Mark A. Prelas

Monsters and Miracles. Horror, Heroes and the Holocaust, by Ira Wesley Kitmacher

Flower of Vlora. Growing up Jewish in Communist Albania, by Anna Kohen

Aftermath: Coming of Age on Three Continents. A Memoir, by Annette Libeskind Berkovits

Not a real Enemy. The True Story of a Hungarian Jewish Man's Fight for Freedom, by Robert Wolf

Zaidy's War. Four Armies, Three Continents, Two Brothers. One Man's Impossible Story of Endurance, by Martin Bodek

The Glassmaker's Son. Looking for the World my Father left behind in Nazi Germany, by Peter Kupfer

The Apprentice of Buchenwald. The True Story of the Teenage Boy Who Sabotaged Hitler's War Machine, by Oren Schneider

Good for a Single Journey, by Helen Joyce

Burying the Ghosts. She escaped Nazi Germany only to have her life torn apart by the woman she saved from the camps: her mother, by Sonia Case

American Wolf. From Nazi Refugee to American Spy. A True Story, by Audrey Birnbaum

Bipolar Refugee. A Saga of Survival and Resilience, by Peter Wiesner

The series **Jewish Children in the Holocaust** consists of the following autobiographies of Jewish children hidden during WWII in the Netherlands:

Searching for Home. The Impact of WWII on a Hidden Child, by Joseph Gosler

See You Tonight and Promise to be a Good Boy! War memories, by Salo Muller

Sounds from Silence. Reflections of a Child Holocaust Survivor, Psychiatrist and Teacher, by Robert Krell

Sabine's Odyssey. A Hidden Child and her Dutch Rescuers, by Agnes Schipper

The Journey of a Hidden Child, by Harry Pila and Robin Black

The series **New Jewish Fiction** consists of the following novels, written by Jewish authors. All novels are set in the time during or after the Holocaust.

The Corset Maker. A Novel, by Annette Libeskind Berkovits

Escaping the Whale. The Holocaust is over. But is it ever over for the next generation? by Ruth Rotkowitz

When the Music Stopped. Willy Rosen's Holocaust, by Casey Hayes

Hands of Gold. One Man's Quest to Find the Silver Lining in Misfortune, by Roni Robbins

The Girl Who Counted Numbers. A Novel, by Roslyn Bernstein

There was a garden in Nuremberg. A Novel, by Navina Michal Clemerson

The Butterfly and the Axe, by Omer Bartov

To Live Another Day. A Novel, Elizabeth Rosenberg

A Worthy Life. Based on a True Story, by Dahlia Moore

The series **Holocaust Heritage** consists of the following memoirs by 2G:

The Cello Still Sings. A Generational Story of the Holocaust and of the Transformative Power of Music, by Janet Horvath

The Fire and the Bonfire. A Journey into Memory, by Ardyn Halter

The Silk Factory: Finding Threads of My Family's True Holocaust Story, by Michael Hickins

---

The series **Holocaust Books for Young Adults** consists of the following novels, based on true stories:

The Boy behind the Door. How Salomon Kool Escaped the Nazis. Inspired by a True Story, by David Tabatsky

Running for Shelter. A True Story, by Suzette Sheft

The Precious Few. An Inspirational Saga of Courage based on True Stories, by David Twain with Art Twain

---

The series **WW2 Historical Fiction** consists of the following novels, some of which are based on true stories:

Mendelevski's Box. A Heartwarming and Heartbreaking Jewish Survivor's Story, by Roger Swindells

A Quiet Genocide. The Untold Holocaust of Disabled Children WW2 Germany, by Glenn Bryant

The Knife-Edge Path, by Patrick T. Leahy

Brave Face. The Inspiring WWII Memoir of a Dutch/German Child, by I. Caroline Crocker and Meta A. Evenbly

When We Had Wings. The Gripping Story of an Orphan in Janusz Korczak's Orphanage. A Historical Novel, by Tami Shem-Tov

Jacob's Courage. Romance and Survival Amidst the Horrors of War, by Charles S. Weinblatt

Want to be an AP book reviewer?

Reviews are very important in a world dominated by the social media and social proof. Please drop us a line if you want to join the *AP review team* and show us at least one review already posted on Amazon for one of our books.
info@amsterdampublishers.com

Made in United States
North Haven, CT
25 August 2023

40726394R00125